What is Freedom?

What is Freedom?

Conversations with Historians, Philosophers, and Activists

Edited by
TOBY BUCKLE

OXFORD
UNIVERSITY PRESS

OXFORD
UNIVERSITY PRESS

Oxford University Press is a department of the University of Oxford. It furthers
the University's objective of excellence in research, scholarship, and education
by publishing worldwide. Oxford is a registered trade mark of Oxford University
Press in the UK and certain other countries.

Published in the United States of America by Oxford University Press
198 Madison Avenue, New York, NY 10016, United States of America.

Library of Congress Cataloging-in-Publication Data
Names: Buckle, Toby, editor.
Title: What is freedom? : Conversations with historians, philosophers, and activists /
edited by Toby Buckle.
Description: First Edition. | New York : Oxford University Press, [2021] |
Includes bibliographical references and index.
Identifiers: LCCN 2021016428 (print) | LCCN 2021016429 (ebook) |
ISBN 9780197572214 (Hardback) | ISBN 9780197572221 (Paperback) |
ISBN 9780197572245 (ePub) | ISBN 9780197572252 (Digital Online)
Subjects: LCSH: Liberty. Classification: LCC JC585 .W44 2021 (print) |
LCC JC585 (ebook) | DDC 323—dc23
LC record available at https://lccn.loc.gov/2021016428
LC ebook record available at https://lccn.loc.gov/2021016429

DOI: 10.1093/oso/9780197572214.001.0001

1 3 5 7 9 8 6 4 2

Paperback printed by Marquis, Canada
Hardback printed by Bridgeport National Bindery, Inc., United States of America

Contents

Foreword   vii
Cécile Fabre

Introduction   1
Toby Buckle

I. HISTORY

1. Ancient Slavery and the Creation of Freedom   13
   Orlando Patterson

2. Slavery and Freedom in Christianity   32
   Dale Martin

3. Freedom in the Liberal Tradition   52
   Michael Freeden

II. PHILOSOPHY

4. Feminism and Freedom   73
   Nancy Hirschmann

5. The Liberty Principle   89
   John Skorupski

6. Freedom as Nondomination   100
   Phillip Pettit

7. Freedom in the Workplace   118
   Elizabeth Anderson

III. ACTIVISM

8. LGBT Liberation   135
   Peter Tatchell

9. Windrush, Racism, and Freedom   149
   Omar Khan

10. Defending EU Liberalism   166
    Ian Dunt

11. Civil Rights Activism   181
    Mary Frances Berry

12. Political Corruption and Citizenship   193
    Zephyr Teachout

Acknowledgments   207
List of Contributors   209
Index   211

Foreword
Cécile Fabre

Philosophy interviews, recorded and made available as podcasts, have become a staple of our discipline, in and outside academia. *Philosophy Bites* paved the way for more specialized series, of which the *Political Philosophy Podcast* series, created and hosted by Toby Buckle, is one of the best. I was the podcast's first interviewee. Our topic, on that occasion, was the ethics of sex work and organ sales. I found Buckle's interviewing style—thoughtful, probing, always willing to allow his guests to go off in unforeseen directions, yet without ever losing sight of the topic at hand—particularly engaging, and agreed to do another two episodes. I am particularly pleased to have been asked to write a Preamble for the volume.

In the last three years, Buckle has turned the series into a "must-listen." Some of the best and most exciting political philosophers in the world have taken part in it. Moreover, Buckle has a broad, humanist understanding of our discipline, which greatly contributes to the appeal of the series. Political philosophy, to him, is not the sole preserve of professional philosophers it is something that all of us can engage in. This is reflected in his choice of interviewees (not all of whom are professional philosophers) and of topics (many of which do not figure on conventional academic syllabi).

This volume gathers transcriptions of twelve of those interviews, all on freedom. It is a unique book. Its format allows us to hear, almost, its contributors' voices, which a collection of essays would not do, and those voices are always powerful, often passionate, sometimes deeply angry. Its interdisciplinarity and its juxtaposition of contributions by scholars and activists is remarkably well suited to its topic.

As Buckle reminds us in his Introduction, the meaning of freedom is far from settled; its history far from linear. It is a "long walk to freedom"—to borrow the title of Nelson Mandela's biography. A walk which, in this book, takes us from slavery—the denial of freedom par excellence—in the Ancient World and early Christianity, to competing conceptions of freedom, or liberty, in 17th- to 20th-century English political thought; from freedom as a contested philosophical concept, to freedom in the contemporary workplace; from freedom as a rallying call for vulnerable workers and LGBT+ campaigners to freedom from gender stereotyping.

It is not possible, within the scope of a Foreword, to do full justice to the range of issues which the book addresses. Still, let me record a few. For a start, it is always worth remembering that freedom—or liberty—used to be equated with licentiousness, disorder, upheaval. Moreover, as the early days of Christianity tell us, it has not always been seen as the antithesis to slavery: to allow Jesus to free us from the earthly bounds of oppression is also, at the same time, to be willing to see him as our master. Those earthly bounds are multifarious: we may tend instinctively to contrast individual freedom with state oppression, but economic oppression, both within the workplace and at the hands of large corporations is, if anything, more keenly felt, by many, than the hands of the state. The struggle for freedom, furthermore, takes many forms, from advocating better sex education as an instrument for liberation from prejudices rooted in gender and sexuality, to chairing the US Civil Rights Commission; from denouncing the corrosive effects of rampant political corruption to denouncing the abusive practices of the Big Data economy. The struggle for freedom takes place in the courtroom, on the pages of newspapers, in military headquarters, in prison, on the street.

We, particularly in what is lazily called "the West," and particularly the privileged among us, take freedom for granted. All twelve interviewees, under Buckle's probing yet never intrusive questioning, do a magnificent job at reminding us that freedom as an idea, as an *ideal*, is not merely to be analyzed and deconstructed; it is lived in, fought for, all too fragile, in constant need of our vigilant protection.

What is Freedom?

Introduction

Toby Buckle

There are moments when we face choices with stakes so high that
they seem to defy rational calculation. In such moments both ordinary people and their leaders will often turn to their ideals for
a guiding light in a seemingly impossible situation. Abraham
Lincoln in the lead-up to the American civil war, facing decisions
which would determine the survival of his country—and the
lives of countless millions—anchored them again and again to a
value: Liberty, or freedom.

It is intriguing then that, anticipating fighting a horrific war in
its name, Lincoln stated that he knew of no good definition for it.
The problem was not simply one of lack of learning on his part; "the
world," he observed, "has never had a good definition of the word
liberty." That the value was strongly held, that people really believed
in it, that they proclaimed, with terrifying sincerity, their willing-
ness kill other human beings for it, did not change this central issue
of meaning.

Lincoln was far from the first to make this observation. It had
been noted throughout the history of his country, one defined
as much as any in human history by its obsession with freedom.
Montesquieu, a philosopher whom the American founders were
greatly influenced by, claimed that "no word" had "had more
significations and meanings" than liberty.

This can seem counterintuitive. When thinking about freedom
many people assume that it is something all people naturally want,

Toby Buckle, *Introduction* In: *What is Freedom?*. Edited by: Toby Buckle, Oxford University Press.
© Oxford University Press 2021. DOI: 10.1093/oso/9780197572214.003.0001

a desire that has been constant in human history. More than that, there is often an assumption, implicit or explicit, that there is some "true" meaning of freedom that has stayed constant over time.

History belies such an assumption. We may have a personal preference for a particular definition of freedom, we may even have good reasons for that preference, but there is no definition that will satisfy the range of ways the term has actually been used in political communication. As Lincoln dryly observed of both slaveholders' and abolitionists' passionate support for freedom, "in using the same word we do not all mean the same thing." John Stuart Mill, a thinker referenced by many of the contributors to this volume, made the point more generally: one of the "mistakes oftenest committed" he claimed, was "supposing that the same name always stands for the same aggregation of ideas."

This pluralism of meaning isn't merely an abstract game, an interesting puzzle for philosophers, of no bearing to the struggles and successes of our day-to-day lives. Those struggles and successes take place in the context of a particular society, culture, and politics. That context did not come from nowhere. We all live in history, our lives are structured by the choices made before us, and freedom is an inescapable part of any account of how our social and political worlds came to be.

The welfare states built by Atlee and FDR were conceived of as vehicles of freedom, their scaling-back in the Thatcher and Reagan revolutions was done in the name of a very different conception of this ideal. Campaigns to improve the lives of historically oppressed racial or ethnic groups often center their cause in ideals of liberation. Freedom as a value has been a part of ending slavery and nominally ending segregation. It was also central to the ideological justification of the structures that made such struggles necessary in the first place: the relative autonomy of the US South and the British and American empires.

We live in a world built by freedom. That many of us live in societies with elected governments, mixed economies, many forms of discrimination, and aspirations to move beyond that discrimination, is, in large part, a consequence of men and women throughout history believing in it.

Over the past few years I've had the great pleasure of taking on the role of an explorer of freedom's many meanings. What it has meant, should mean, and could mean. In my role as host of the Political Philosophy Podcast I've interviewed many of the world's leading historians, philosophers, and theorists, as well as activists, journalists, and politicians.

Freedom is a concept the podcast has spent a great deal of time on. I've interviewed dozens of people, from a huge variety of backgrounds and ideological perspectives, on the topic. This volume brings together some of those interviews, together with others recorded specifically for this work. Putting together this introduction I'm still somewhat taken aback by how incredible the list of contributors is, and how uniquely qualified to discuss the topic they are. From world-renowned historians, theorists, and philosophers, to activists, journalists, and politicians, these are people who have genuinely changed both the world and our understanding of it. While there are other books that feature collections of articles on freedom from within a particular field, this volume is unique in bringing together such a range of perspectives.

The choice to aim for this diversity of views, as well as the choice of which views to include, was shaped by my background as a progressive activist. For much of the past 10 years I've worked for left-wing politicians, human rights organizations, and a variety of progressive campaigns. My interest in political philosophy comes from trying to understand the work ideas, values, and ideologies do in the world, how they have shaped our lives, and how they can point the way to better futures. My belief is that these questions are mutually informing and a mature understanding of any value, in this case freedom, can only come from considering it from a variety of angles.

The book opens with history, specifically with thinkers who argue that freedom was created in response to specific social and political circumstances, that it has changed and adapted in response to different circumstances, and that its meaning has always been contested by different groups and belief systems throughout its history. It starts by looking at the origins of Freedom. Challenging the view that freedom is a universal or natural aspiration, Orlando Patterson argues that, as a value, it was invented in the classical world in response to particular social and political circumstances—namely the advent of large-scale slave societies in Greece and Rome. Dale Martin and I discuss how these Greek and Roman understandings of slavery and freedom were incorporated and adapted by the Christian tradition, looking particularly at the person of St Paul. Finally, Michael Freeden looks at freedom within liberalism, arguing that it has always been contested within that tradition between individualists and progressives.

Even when considering history there is not a universal approach on how to look at freedom. In this section the reader is presented with three very different ways of approaching freedom in history: that of the historical sociologist, the critical historian, and the theorist of language. The point is to introduce the reader to a set of tools: This is what this way of thinking is, this what it looks like in action, this is what seems to follow from it.

Just as the volume seeks to challenge the assumption of a stable meaning through history, it also seeks to show that freedom is still contested, that our dominant understandings should not be assumed to be the settled, or even default meaning.

It is certainly true that a conception of freedom that consists of individuals being left alone—"nonconstraint" in the language of philosophers—has become the most common meaning, particularly for the most powerful in society. While there are some thinkers who would take this definition in different directions (left libertarians for instance), it is most commonly evoked in actual political discourse by the political right—conservative politicians, economic libertarians, business interests in their defense of "free market" institutions, and a variety of reactionary movements.

Opponents of changes in our lives because of the coronavirus, such as masking requirements or shutting down venues, for example, have claimed these restrictions are grotesque violations of our freedom, seem to understand the value in this sense. Restrictions on American's ability to own guns have likewise been portrayed as assaults on this sacred ideal. Plutocrats at the top of our economy indignantly portray (and no doubt genuinely feel that) all regulation of their business activities are necessarily a restriction on their freedom, not to mention on the "free market" system in general.

This is not however the entire story of freedom today: those who would seek to regulate plutocrats will point to the lack of freedom their workers enjoy. They will bitterly condemn the ability of the super-rich to make unlimited contributions to politicians as an assault on our democracy, and hence an undermining of our democratic freedom. Similarly, those in social justice movements often conceive of their ultimate goal as the liberation of historically oppressed groups from power structures that systematically disenfranchise, exclude, and marginalize them. Clearly their vision of liberty is very different from that of the plutocrat or anti-mask activist.

The philosophy section of this book considers a number of alternate understandings to the dominant view. Nancy Hirschmann provides the reader with an introduction to the distinction philosophers draw between positive and negative liberty. She argues that our understanding of what it is to be free must take into account additional factors beyond individuals being left alone. She illustrates this case with respect to women's freedom: their ability to make choices in a society where people often think of them, and what they should be doing, differently than they do men. Another vision for how we might think about freedom in the modern world, the liberty principle, is presented to us by John Skorupski. This is an account that is still strongly individualistic, but grounds that individualism on the idea of self-development, as opposed to simple libertarian rights protection. Taking a different path, Philip Pettit introduces us to the idea that freedom is about who has the power to influence your life, even if they don't use it. Finally, and following this, Elizabeth Anderson asks us if freedom requires us simply to limit the power of governments, or if it might also require us to look at the power employers have over our lives.

Just as there is not one way to practice history, there is not one way to practice philosophy. The thinkers interviewed in this section all construct their theories in different ways. Again, the point is to simply introduce the reader to different tools; different ways that they can start thinking about what freedom ought to mean in a sustained way.

The final section of the volume brings you the voices of people who are in the business of trying to effect real political change. Once again, the volume seeks to challenge, to impart a sort of negative knowledge. All of the contributors to this section I think would want to challenge the assumption that the economically developed representative democracies many of us live in are societies that have largely achieved freedom. Beyond that, many of these chapters challenge the assumption that achieving freedom is something self-sustaining, that once achieved it will take care of itself. Rather they argue, often forcefully, that its protection requires our constant attention.

The first two interviews, with Peter Tatchell and Omar Kahn, explore freedom as a goal of social movements from the perspective of LGBTQ rights and anti-racism respectively. What I like about these chapters is they show how activists, at least at a high level, face very similar questions to philosophers: should we aim for equality or freedom? Should we focus on the individual or the group, or both? The difference is the environment in which they have to work out answers: Instead of asking if their account of these values passes the philosophical tests of consistency and rigor of argument, they must ask will it persuade, will it motivate people, does it imply an agenda that is realistic or aspirational? Activists think about these questions with just as much seriousness as philosophers, but they are forced, by the nature of their work, to think about them in different ways. Far from being a bad thing, this is to the benefit of the student of politics trying to understand freedom: it gives us an opportunity to see the same concept from a plurality of perspectives, different windows onto the same aquarium.

In the final three interviews we look at what is involved in the maintenance and expansion of freedom from the perspective of different types of political actors: journalists, campaigners, politicians, and citizens. Ian Dunt discusses defending liberal freedom in the context of Brexit, with particular reference to the obligations of journalists to explain what is happening and what is at stake for the public. Mary Frances Berry draws on history and her own experience to offer advice on how protest movements can succeed in realizing their goals. Finally, Zephyr Teachout argues that to maintain a free democratic society we need to produce public-facing politicians and active citizens—and identifies structures that allow political corruption as a key threat to that.

Throughout this collection the interviews all pursue different directions. The interviewees all bring different experiences and perspectives. As such the volume as a whole does not point the reader in the direction of a single clear answer, an anchor point in a complex political world. Nor does it proclaim a whiggish faith in the inevitability of our final victory. The hope offered, such as it is, is that if our current frameworks have proved inadequate to the moment these can be set aside—and in doing so can open our eyes to the richness of the resources available to us.

What comes through in the volume however, in the absence of final answers, is what such answers might look like. What developing a definition of freedom, and how to realize it, would involve. One great virtue of putting together discussions from such eclectic sources is we can see not only the different paths but the commonalities between them. Indeed, as editor of a uniquely varied volume, I was struck by how often the interviewees came back to two questions: how we think about our relationship with history, and how we think about ourselves.

The historians in this volume certainly had something to say about our relationship with history, but so did the philosophers. Every single one of the contributors to the activism section grounded their views deeply in history. Indeed, anyone who has spent time with leading activists will tell you that they're not just interested in history, they're obsessed with it. How we relate to our history is a perennial fascination for reflective campaigners; what can we learn from it, how are we shaped by it, should we focus on the progress we have made, or the evils that remain?

The other big takeaway for me in putting together this volume is how every contributor, often without any prompting, referenced in their answers, implicitly or explicitly, questions of how we see ourselves. What our account of human nature is. What features of it do we give priority—the individualist parts, the choice-making parts, the communal parts, the dependent or vulnerable parts? Do we assume that people are primarily selfish or altruistic, or some combination? Do we desire equality with others, or power and domination over them? Do we assume that people's core attributes are fixed, or that they can change and develop? If they can change can this be done *to* them by others, or is it something they must do for themselves?

Not only did the philosophical accounts of freedom often make reference to such questions, but the questions came up again and again in my conversations about history and activism. This collection offers us a fascinating opportunity to see what a biologist might call convergent evolution: from very different starting points, very different people were drawn to the same questions. It is left to the reader to consider whose answers they find most satisfying, or to what degree the answers might complement or contrast with one another.

The collection does not need to be read in order; any individual chapter can be appreciated by itself. I include a very short introduction to the topic and the interviewee before each chapter, and a few recommendations for further reading after. The goal is to make each conversation function as a self-contained unit. If however, the reader does work through these conversations from start to finish they will be taken on a journey that starts with seeing that freedom is an interesting and important topic, discovering that many of our implicit assumptions about it are wrong, and realizing that dropping those assumptions reveals a rich pluralism of resources that speak to our current intellectual and political moment.

The claim is not that answers about our ultimate ideals are easy to find, simply that they are there to be found, and may be there in one of our culture's oldest, most elusive, and, in some respects, strangest values: freedom.

PART I
HISTORY

1

Ancient Slavery and the Creation
of Freedom

Orlando Patterson

One of the books that has most influenced how I think about history is *Freedom in the Making of Western Culture* by Orlando Patterson. A magisterial work, it carries the reader through several millennia of history, pausing to give us vivid details of particular periods, while never losing focus on its provocative central thesis. It's a work I recommend to everyone, partly for the quality of the writing, but mainly for how challenging it is to what we assume about our history, and how we see our relationship to it.

In it Patterson argues that freedom, far from being universal, or even "discovered," was invented. Not only that, but that its invention was brought about by the institution of large-scale slave society. And that, as such, the value that has been a guiding light for so many societies, particularly in the west, has its roots in some of history's most evil institutions, and the experience of the people who were victims of them.

Orlando Patterson is John Cowles Professor of Sociology at Harvard University. He previously held faculty appointments at the University of the West Indies and the London School of Economics. He is the author of numerous academic papers and six major academic books, including *Slavery and Social Death* (1982), *Freedom in the Making of Western Culture* (1991), *The Ordeal of Integration* (1997), and *The Cultural Matrix: Understanding Black Youth* (2015), as well as three novels.

Orlando Patterson, *Ancient Slavery and The Creation of Freedom* In: *What is Freedom?*.
Edited by: Toby Buckle, Oxford University Press. © Oxford University Press 2021.
DOI: 10.1093/oso/9780197572214.003.0002

A public intellectual, Professor Patterson was, for eight years, Special Advisor for Social Policy and Development to Prime Minister Michael Manley of Jamaica. He was a founding member of Cultural Survival, one of the leading advocacy groups for the rights of indigenous peoples, and was for several years a board member of Freedom House, a major civic organization for the promotion of freedom and democracy around the world. He has published widely in journals of opinion and the national press including the *New York Times*, *Time Magazine*, *Newsweek*, *The Public Interest*, *The New Republic*, and *The Washington Post*.

He is the recipient of many awards, including the National Book Award for Nonfiction, which he won in 1991 for his book on freedom; the Distinguished Contribution to Scholarship Award of the American Sociological Association; the Ralph Bunche Award for the best book on pluralism from the American Political Science Association, as co-winner; and the Anisfield-Wolf Book Award for Lifetime Achievement. He holds honorary degrees from several universities, including the University of Chicago, UCLA, and La Trobe University in Australia. He was awarded the Order of Distinction by the Government of Jamaica in 1999.

I was fortunate enough to spend some time with professor Patterson and record a multipart podcast series on the history of freedom. It was a wide-ranging conversation, covering almost the entire history of freedom, that I enjoyed immensely. This opening chapter brings together some of the key material from that conversation with the goal of giving an accessible overview of Patterson's thesis on the creation of freedom.

In *Freedom and the Making of Western Culture* you write:
"Armed with the weapons of a historical sociologist I had gone in search of a man-killing wolf called slavery; to my dismay I kept finding the tracks of a lamb called freedom. A lamb that stared back at me, on our first furtive encounters in the foothills of the Western past, with strange, uninnocent eyes."

Can you explain that, how did you come to study freedom?

Growing up I was existentially involved with the problem of freedom and of slavery. I grew up in colonial Jamaica during the decolonization period. So freedom was in the air in a collective sense, of freedom from the British colonial rule. But also as I grew up, I had a great interest in slavery. In fact, in the decolonization of colonial education, which had originally been focused on the wonders and grandeur of the British empire, we finally were being taught about the real past. I became almost obsessed with the problem of slavery, because it increasingly became obvious that Jamaican and Caribbean problems are weighed down heavily by the slave and the plantation past. In my case, I grew up literally surrounded by plantations.

So the ghosts of the past are part of my childhood. I knew that the study of slavery was going to be essential in any understanding of society. My interest in freedom however started rather early with a paradox I had as a young, colonial kid. Every year, on the 24th of May, we celebrated Empire Day. If you can imagine, all over the half of the world that the British ruled, little schoolchildren were waiving the Union Jack. We got a day off, so we loved it, for the day off, and for the ice cream. We would sing national British songs, and one of the ones we sang before we got to the anthem was *Rule Britannia*.

"Britons never, never, never will be slaves."

Yeah! Even as a ten-year-old I always kind of scratched my head at that little line. Because who ever threatened the British with being slaves? They were the ones that went around enslaving half the world, especially in my neck of the woods. So it was very strange that the imperialists were saying that Britons never will be slaves. What is going on? Clearly the definition of being free is that you're never a slave. That's when the idea was planted in my head, singing this song every 24th of May.

Then my first academic works were on slavery in Jamaica, which had one of the most cruel forms of slavery anywhere in history, but which also had (partly for that reason) one of the highest traditions of slave revolts in the name of freedom. You've heard of the Haitian slave revolt, which is often celebrated as the first successful slave revolt, but in fact, that's not quite accurate. The first successful slave revolt was the long strain of revolts from 1655, when the British captured the Island, and 1740, between the British and runaway slaves, known as maroons. Eventually the British sued for peace and did something quite extraordinary (extraordinary in the history of slave societies); they actually granted them their freedom, a state within a state, and their own government.

The idea of fighting for one's freedom remained as an essential feature of Jamaican life. The slave revolts of 1832 were critical in pushing the British parliament to pass the abolition act, but Jamaicans have been rebelling ever since, even afterward.

So I've always been preoccupied with the problem of slavery and of freedom, and the connection was there lurking in my mind, between me singing on the 24th as well as the rebellious nature, the love of freedom, in Jamaica. Then, when I wrote *Slavery and Social Death*, in the course of that research, it became increasingly clear to me that the act of manumission is the foundation of an institutionalized notion of freedom.

What is slavery?
That was essential problem of *Slavery and Social Death*. I'd written about it, at great length, in *The Sociology of Slavery*, a study of Jamaica. Then I saw that it was widespread throughout the world, Jamaicans weren't unique, or the Caribbean peoples, or the modern world. So my question is, what exactly was this shared experience?

You begin with the famous United Nations definition of 1926, which emphasizes ownership. Essentially this is the Roman legal definition of slavery as the ownership of one person by another, the legal possession of another person. That became, and that still is for many people, the fundamental view of slavery.

But I immediately came upon a problem using that definition for the simple reason that in many situations human beings are owned by others and are clearly not slaves. Even the language we use in, for instance, many marital arrangements, women are literally sold. Anthropologists have always known this. They use all kinds of euphemisms to get around the fact; they call it a bride price, or a bride sale, or an exchange, but it's, in many societies, a sale. More interestingly, even advanced societies, we sell bodies and it's only the fiction of the separability of a person's services from their body that allows us to deny this. But the term is used, quite openly. In professional sports we say: "Joe Namath was just sold from this team to that team."

So the property concept struck me as not very useful if we are to understand the real meaning of slavery, which I saw as more meaningfully understood as a relation of domination; the most extreme form of the relation of domination. Obviously there's a continuum, but this is absolute domination of one person by another. In which violence or the threat of violence is central. In which degradation and dishonoring is critical. And in which a cultural idea exists that the slave does not belong, does not belong to the society in which you live, does not belong to the society from which he or she has been taken. She is a genealogical isolate, she does not belong to her parents or her grandparents, and has no rights of belonging herself. Her kids do not belong to her. That idea is central to all experiences of slavery from far more so than any notion of property.

How far back does slavery date, and how widespread across different cultures has it been?

One of the most extraordinary discoveries of archeologists and students of preliterate or small scale societies is that when trading begins, it's usually trading in people. This pattern, that early trade, especially with people who have nothing else, tends to involve enslaving people, persistent even in western societies. So the Vikings, which we tend to glorify as traders and great sailors, what were they trading? They were slave traders, they were trading those poor Irish women.

So the trading of persons is something that's chronic in human societies. This thing has been with human beings from the very beginning, and it's still with us.

It seems like there must have been multiple, independent inventions of slavery, given that we observe it in all of the different continents. One thing I wonder about is does the fact that so many people invented the same institution, say something fundamental about human nature? Is there some core impulse we have that causes us to enslave?

We naturally have a tendency to want to dominate others. What's interesting however is that early societies seem to have gone out of their way to prevent the absolute domination of one person by another. In kin-based societies you have a situation in which the best position you could be in is to be embedded in interlocking networks. That's what kinship is. You always have a protector, not just your immediate father, but your uncles, your uncle's uncle, or what have you, depending on if it's patrilineal or matrilineal.

Slavery, in a sense, broke through that. It was the only way in which someone could directly dominate someone in these societies, which had these countervailing networks of interaction. So we find slavery occurring over and over. And you get this even in the language. If you look at the European languages what is the original word "freedom"? It's very intriguing and immediately suggests how the idea emerged. Freedom meant originally to be "among the beloved," "we who are not slaves." From the very beginning, in the deepest roots of the Indo-European language, it was defined in negative terms.

What was the role of slaves in early societies? Primarily they had noneconomic functions, right?

Yes, very often slaves were an economic burden. In some cases among some nomadic herdsmen you may get slaves being used to do the really dirty work, but by and large the level of surplus involved was such that the keeping of a slave is usually more a liability than an asset. Certainly, among hunter-gatherers it made no sense. Even among early horticulturalists, the slave was usually an economic burden. They were being used for honorific purposes, for sexual purposes, and for reproductive purposes.

Could you explain what you mean by honorific purposes?

Take the case of the Tupinambra of northeastern Brazil. They were a pretty warlike group of people, so honor was central to their whole system and capturing the enemy was the height of gaining honor. They were a hunter-gathering group mainly, and they lived very well. They were fishers and there was an abundance of fish, so they didn't need slaves for economic purposes, what they needed them for was honorific purposes.

After capture the slave was assigned to one master and was actually well fed and looked after until, of course, the moment came for his sacrifice, which the entire community saw as literally consuming the vitality and the life force of the enemy. That was their main function. There were a few of them, and they treated them like fattening one favorite calf, until the movement in which they were consumed in ritualistic cannibalism.

But this is true of many other societies, whether they're used for cannibalistic purposes or not, the important point is that the honor gained from owning a slave was critical, as well as the degradation of the slave. I've called it a parasitic form of honor, in the sense that you gain honor in the degradation of the slaves, in that there lives another human being, who is totally in your control, who is literally an extension of you.

And that idea did not end with primitive societies, it went right through. It was very important in Roman society, where it had economic consequences. The degradation, the idea of the other person being an extension had important consequences: while we think of Romans, quite rightly, as great legal scholars, they had one interesting failure and that is that the law of agency was not very well developed.

The way in which the Romans, in the absence of this legal principle, get around it is by owning slaves. So if you are in Rome and you have business with someone in Corinth there's no way in which you could sue them or complete a transaction. If a lawyer turned up they could say, "we want to see Cicero right here, and I'm not going to take your signature." If your slave turned up however, that was you, he was literally an extension of you. So you can do business, and that's why slaves and freedmen became so critically important.

But although both had slavery, you've argued that only in Greece and Rome did freedom emerge. In early societies, or even nonwestern societies prior to contact with the west, people didn't want to be slaves but would never have thought of not being one as a positive social value. Just as we don't want to be homeless but would never say the purpose of our society is nonhomelessness.

Exactly. The idea (which is so common that it's hardwired into us) that everyone, given the chance, would desire freedom is simply not true. There are many, many societies where it did not happen, where indeed it is viewed as an abomination.

I got several of my Asian students to do etymological work for me on the origins of "freedom." "Freedom" is now in all languages, but that's just because of the influence of the west. It was an interesting exercise to examine what are the roots of the idea. My favorite imaginary story is this: Many dictionaries of eastern languages were written by missionaries at the end of their failed attempts. So after thirty years of proselytizing without anyone listening, they say "we must do something useful, and get a dictionary of this language." So they go around and you ask people, "what's your word for cat?," "what's your word for cat?," and so forth. And then you get to concepts. I always imagine an interaction in which it's "okay, here's a more difficult idea, but tell me what your word for freedom is?"

The response has invariably been, "what do you mean?' So the missionary then would have to say, "well, I'll tell you what I mean by it, and you tell me what your word is.' What's very interesting is, when the light bulb goes off, the word given is usually what the Chinese give them; the word meaning licentiousness. The same thing happens in Japan, it means irresponsible, it means selfishness, and so on. The literal meaning of freedom translated is always something negative, because people just thought that this was not a good idea.

The question then arises, how did this happen? The idea is associated with one of the most horrible experiences, as you mention, it's like making not being homeless a central value. How does an idea with such a degraded pedigree, associated with the most degraded people, and the most degraded condition, become the preeminent value in the west? (Assuming that's how it happened, many people deny that true freedom could have anything to do with slavery.) That's where Greece comes in, and later Rome. It's in Athens we know most about it although it could have happened in several of Greek polises.

I want to avoid a triumphalist narrative about Athens inventing "western civilization." That framing is often used in the service of some quite ugly ideological projects. However Athens, or at least Greece as a whole, in terms of the institutions and concepts that they come up with, really is strikingly unusual sociohistorically.

Yeah, this is my biggest problem having grown up as a colonial, with a colonial education. We were taught all civilization, anything worthwhile in human thought, begins with the Greeks and, of course, culminated with the British. It was an idea I strongly resisted for most of my undergraduate and later years, I said that's a whole lot of European ethnocentrism.

But facts are facts. It's just quite clear that the idea of freedom did not emerge in other societies which had slavery. Even though they have words for it, as a concept, it was not seen as important.

So how on earth did this idea become important? It's in Athens in which we have a lot of data (some version of it may well have emerged in some of the other cities). There is this very close relationship between the rise of slavery and the rise of freedom consciousness in Athens.

You can trace this very closely to its culmination in the latter half the fifth century BC, the development of this idea as important. Now, interestingly, the revulsion of this idea being associated with slavery also existed in Greece. And here's where things get complicated, because the elite scholars such as Plato, who we read, and to whose work we are indebted to for our knowledge of Greece, were similarly disdainful of the idea of freedom in a secular external sense.

But the fact that Plato is disdainful of any understanding of freedom that would involve democracy shows that the idea is doing significant work in his world. What had changed in Greece that caused it to develop there and not elsewhere?

The invention of large-scale slave society, as opposed to simply slaveholding societies which you had all over the world from primitive times. What emerged for the first time in history was this unusual phenomenon of a society whose economy, and certainly a society whose elite, depended entirely on slaves.

That itself is a very unusual thing. Elites usually find ways of exploiting the masses of their own societies. It's very unusual for an elite to suddenly find itself without its exploited masses. That we can track to a very important series of developments in the late seventh century BC: there was large-scale debt bondage in Athens from the eighth century going right down to the late seventh century and there is evidence that the population was on the verge of rebellion. It's to avert this that Solon the so-called liberator (he was liberating more his class than the masses) accepted the abolition of debt bondage, which then created a labor crisis for the elite.

The way in which the elite solved the problem was to bring in slaves. Throughout the course of the sixth century, you'll find this development; the bringing in of a large number of people from outside into society. As a result, the society became increasingly dependent on slavery; dependent on slaves for the silver mines (which had the most horrendous form of slavery), for the home farms, and also for the urban economy.

Those wonderful statues, those wonderful buildings, all the public works, were done by slaves. So the urban economy, which is the heart of the civilization, was totally dependent on slavery and that never happened before.

So you've got this development of large-scale slavery, how is that generative of freedom as a social value?

Before Greece, slavery was marginal to the economy. In the ancient near eastern societies slaves were not important at all. They had corvée labor, they had peasants, slaves were primarily domestic.

Now you had this complete dependence on slavery. Especially in an advanced urban economy like Greece, or later Rome, that creates a real motivation problem. If you had a motivation problem before, you had an even bigger one now. The way in which you motivated slaves was through the method of manumission, of offering them the prospect of freedom. In spite of all its horrors, there's a very high rate of manumission in Greece and there's an even higher rate in Rome.

In fact, one estimate is that by the age of thirty-six the average slave in Rome who worked hard could expect to buy his freedom. That was essential for the system. So now you have a large number of people, many of whom are highly educated and highly skilled, who were desiring one thing and one thing only, and would all be motivated by getting that thing. And that is the freedom which came from not being a slave.

So you had this idea becoming critical for a critical mass of the population which you never had before. These are not just domestics, these were architects, these were policemen, these were bureaucrats.

Then what you have is another important development which explains how the elites got into it. Not only were they slave owners, and therefore we're encouraging this notion of freedom, but you also had a threat of enslavement to the population as a whole from foreign powers. The near defeat by the Persians, and the escape from mass enslavement to them, became very important, especially for the elite, who then began to celebrate freedom in an even more collective way.

But they were the ones who, at the same time, were also encouraging freedom among the people they were enslaving within their own societies. So you had this remarkable convergence of elite celebration of how they succeeded in preventing Greece from becoming slaves and the development of the idea of freedom among the people they were enslaving and freeing in the last half of the fifth century.

This is where my idea of freedom becomes somewhat more complex than a simple escape from slavery, because what do you have in the slave situation? You have the slave, you have the slave owner, and you have those that were never enslaved. Those who were never enslaved begin to define their condition as a desirable one, that of not being a slave. These are the hoplites, the free citizens, the small farmers who had been freed from debt bondage way back by Solon. They had already begun to cherish an idea of not being bonded. When you brought in a lot of slaves, it was even more reinforced that "we" are not them; the slaves, the barbarians or non-Greek. "We" are this superior group who are the nonslaves, in other words, the free.

So you had a convergence of forces: This large mass of free, proud, nonslave small farmers who were celebrating the fact that they were not slaves, both historically in that they were no longer debt bonded, as well as not being these people brought in as slaves.

You had the notion of freedom from the elite who celebrated the fact that they were powerful, and power became an important element in defining what the slave masters viewed as freedom. The idea of being in absolute control, being able to defend your country, as well as being able to exercise power within your own society.

And of course there was the slave, for whom it was simply a matter of getting the hell out of this horrible situation. In other words, the negative freedom.

So what emerged, from the very beginning, is a tripartite idea of freedom: You'll have the slaves' idea: freedom is not being under the domination of another person. The idea emerging among the mass of the free farmers: you are free by virtue of being part of the collective entity, which is Greek, which will not be dominated by anyone else. And you had the elite idea of freedom as power.

It's important to recognize these ideas emerging together. It's not just the slave's negative idea, indeed the elites often may look down on that. Although they recognized that if you want to be free in the sense of exercising power, you have to be free in the sense of not being under the domination of another. And then you have the idea of being free in the sense of sharing in a collective power and not being part of a despised group.

It's a remarkable development, not only in the sense that freedom became such a powerful idea, but it had this rather complex tripartite feature about it in which slavery was central. They were all there in the seeds of freedom. You have to understand how then the slave owner became involved in celebrating this idea, as well as the ex-slave, as well as people who are neither slave owners or slave, but who took pride in the fact that they were among the beloved.

Here's something I wonder about: Let's say Athens really is unique in creating freedom as a social value (as a consequence of being a

brutal slave society). Let's also say freedom is highly consequential; this value is going to play a central role in the development of later societies and institutions, as well as the conquest and enslavement of most of the world (freedom is central to the ideological justification of Roman, British, and American imperialism). Is all of that, the good and evil alike, contingent on these unusual social developments in a small city-state which may well not have survived?

Put simply, if the Athenians had been defeated at Marathon (which everyone expected them to be) does the rest of history just not happen? Or happen in such a radically different way as to be beyond our ability to conceptualize?

Let's say western history. Things are happening in China and in Japan which are different, but western history, yes. I'm prepared to admit that developments here could have gone in very different ways if not for Marathon, and maybe if not for other developments too.

But let's test this idea by looking at what happened in Sicily when the actual Athenian army was totally defeated. It didn't lead to the collapse of civilization. But then one could say they were not defeated by Persians, that these were, in a way, fellow Greeks.

Also Athens itself physically survived. They were scared, but still there.

Yes. As I said, it took me quite some time to acknowledge what the facts seem to be. A lot of people don't accept this, so one person who I greatly respect who has been somewhat critical is Amartya Sen, the very eminent philosopher and economist. He refuses to accept this reading of history and freedom and has written lucidly and powerfully on freedom himself.

He has stated flatly that it happened in India. But the examples he gives are rather odd. I mean, I've said to him, look, I'm not saying that the idea that it's good not to be a slave didn't exist, in the same way that the simple idea of not being homeless exists today. It's such a simple notion that anywhere slaves existed, they would want to be free. But that's not what I'm talking about. What I'm talking about is this very complex, very powerful valorization of a cultural trope, a cultural value, which then becomes the preeminent value in the civilization.

There's nothing like this anywhere else in the world. Some Indian sage might get up one day and say "this might be a good idea," someone might say, "it's in this ancient Sanskrit text." That misses the whole point; you have this extraordinary valorization of an idea. That happened only once, in ancient Athens. It didn't happen elsewhere, even in other societies that had slaves.

Why didn't it happen elsewhere?
You did not have large-scale slave societies. Sir Moses Finley made this critical distinction between slaveholding societies, which you get everywhere, and slave societies. Societies that become almost completely dependent, certainly an elite becomes totally dependent, on slaves. That is a crucial new structure in ancient Athens. Nowhere else did that exist.

If the Greeks had been, to take your counterfactual, defeated at Marathon, what would have happened to them is they would have been made subject people. They may have carted off and planted somewhere else, like the Jews in captivity, or made subjects in their own lands in which they paid tribute.

Most of the world before Athens did not find slavery a good idea as a way of exploiting people. The Chinese built great structures, great walls, elaborate irrigation works, from other sources of labor. They used the corvée system. There was slavery in Han China, and the Koreans had a fair degree of slavery. But, by and large, in most eastern societies and all near eastern societies the individual or

enslavement of people on a large scale was not found to be a very
efficient way of exploiting people.

**If Athens, or the Greeks generally, were unique in both their de-
pendence on slavery, and their celibration of freedom, how do
those ideas change when they're taken up by Rome?**

Rome was the greatest of all large-scale slave societies, and that
includes modern slavery. What is extraordinary about Rome is
not only a continuation of this, but this is when freedom becomes
a mass value. The interesting thing about the Greeks is that they
love freedom but they largely wanted to keep it to themselves. If you
read Aristotle on barbarians, he thinks they're just not worthy of
this wonderful thing.

Freedom broke out very soon from the Greeks however. There's
a wonderful passage in Philo, the Jewish philosopher of the
Hellenistic period, in which he describes going to a performance of
Euripides. He said that at the end of the play people broke out into
great applause at the end, celebrating the term "freedom" and how
wonderful it was. This is even before Rome. What happens with
Rome is what I call the universalization of the idea.

Rome was this large-scale slave society with strongly emphasized
freedom. You had slavery penetrating every section of the society, and
the main meaning of freedom in Rome was libertas, which means not
to be a slave. Slavery was a mode of production in the latifundia, the
plantations. You know, one of the texts I had to read studying Latin
was Cato, De agri cultura, which was essentially a manual of how to
run a slave plantation. Can you imagine, as a little colonial schoolboy,
reading this text? It was taught with no sense of irony.

That's an amazing image.
Yeah. It's one of the things that's rendered to my obsession with this
subject; thinking "how is this possible?"

Anyway, slavery is also found in the urban economy in Rome, as
well as in the entire lower section of the civil service, the only part

of Rome which slaves weren't involved with was the military. You had it in the Imperial court, the freedmen at one time, especially under the Claudian emperors, virtually dominated the Imperial household. One of the best documented aspects of Roman history is the vast number of freedmen who basically ran the economy and sometimes created and ran entire colonies, such as the rebuilding of Corinth. It had been destroyed, was revived by freedmen, and became the most extraordinary slave society run by ex-slaves with a high proportion of the population enslaved.

The remarkable thing about Rome was that, unlike even Greece, freedmen celebrated the fact that they were once slaves and were freed.

Sort of like Americans like rags to riches stories. Billionaires love bragging about their humble origins.

Exactly. It's a good parallel. They're not ashamed of it. Reading some of these monumental inscriptions, it's just amazing; "I Claudius (or whatever) was, born so-and-so, and became a slave of so-and-so, and on this date achieved my freedom." They celebrated the idea! In a way in which you didn't even get in Greece.

Although some of the nobles had a kind of "old money/new money" snobbery about them.

There is that dynamic, but they couldn't do it with a straight face for too long because by the first-century Latin culture had been so powerfully influenced by former slaves, especially from Greece. Much of Roman civilization was this sort of a replication, especially Roman philosophy, but also a bunch of Roman culture. So they may have been snotty, and they did behave that way, but it was hard to maintain, even in high culture.

Look at the role of Horace, he was a son of a slave, and became the pinnacle of Roman culture. His writing was a powerful influence in the development of the language. You get it also in the theater early on in the plays of Terrence and Plautus, they're likely both ex-slaves. So the whole civilization was permeated by people who were once slaves who wanted to be free, and freedom then became the dominant idea. What also persists is the notion of freedom as power as well as freedom as liberation. What a freedman wants to do most, once he gets his freedom, and especially if he's rich, is he wants to own slaves. That wasn't seen as a contradiction to the idea of freedom as not only escape from slavery, but also having power over others. The idea that got muted in Rome was of course the idea of freedom as democracy, the freedom of the free man.

There's these two grand historical narratives. One, which you might call the western triumphalist narrative, and the other, which is a reaction against it, that wants to go back and point out all the evil that led us to this point.
What I love about your work is the interplay between the two. Am I right in thinking that's a central theme in your work: that history is not the triumph of good over evil, or evil over good, but a demonstration of their tragic interdependence?

Absolutely. Yes. "Out of evil cometh good," but also a lot of future evils. It goes right through to modern times. One of the big paradoxes (which it's so obvious that I'm always amazed that people fail to appreciate it) is the American revolution and its creation of this great democratic system, the Declaration of Independence, and the Constitution, which Americans still celebrate as one of the great moments in the history of freedom (which sadly it is) were all the work of slave owners.

American historians have gnashed their teeth and teared their hair. They think "oh, we've got this great invention, this great contribution to society, Isn't it a tragedy? Isn't it sad that this was done by large-scale slave owners?'

And you want to say that slavery isn't a blot on an otherwise noble history, it's an instrumental part of it, one of the process that led us to this point.

It's instrumental to it! It's not an accident that it was a slave owner in Virginia who led the revolution and wrote the Constitution. It's not an accident that the slave South celebrates freedom more than any other part of the United States. This contradiction is an inherent part of western history, and most historians are very reluctant to accept this. The narrative has got to be good or bad. What I'm saying is that often in the worst of evils you find good emerging, and some of the worst tragedies emerged from the best of intentions.

Further Reading

Patterson, Orlando. *Slavery and Social Death*. Harvard University Press 1982.
Patterson, Orlando. *Freedom in the Making of Western Culture*. Basic Books 1991.

2

Slavery and Freedom in Christianity

Dale Martin

Freedom as a value has been used to articulate not only political visions but also religious ones. The language of slavery and freedom permeate the New Testament: In the writings of Paul, the earliest sources we have from the Christian movement, they are used as metaphors in ways that may seem highly counterintuitive to modern readers. This conversation aims to introduce readers to the historical study of Paul, how and why he used this language, and what that can tell us about his conception of freedom.

I've heard it said that good communicators make you feel that *they* are smart when you listen to them. Great communicators make you feel like *you* are smart for following along. By this metric Dale Martin's communication in his speaking, writing, and even conversation, is absolutely masterful. He has an ability to make the minutia of historical method feel like a thrilling detective story of which you are a part, to feel as if you are really getting inside the heads of ancient writers (or at least the best construction of them that we in the modern world are capable of).

Dale B. Martin specializes in New Testament and Christian Origins, including attention to social and cultural history of the Greco-Roman world. Before joining the Yale faculty in 1999, he taught at Rhodes College and Duke University. His books include: *Slavery as Salvation: The Metaphor of Slavery in Pauline Christianity*; *The Corinthian Body*; *Inventing Superstition: From the Hippocratics to the Christians*; *Sex and the Single Savior: Gender and Sexuality in Biblical Interpretation*; *Pedagogy of the Bible: An*

Dale Martin, *Slavery and Freedom in Christianity* In: *What is Freedom?*. Edited by: Toby Buckle, Oxford University Press. © Oxford University Press 2021. DOI: 10.1093/oso/9780197572214.003.0003

Analysis and Proposal; New Testament History and Literature; and most recently, *Biblical Truths: The Meaning of Scripture in the Twenty-First Century.*

He has edited several books, including (with Patricia Cox Miller), *The Cultural Turn in Late Ancient Studies: Gender, Asceticism, and Historiography.* He was an associate editor for the revision and expansion of the *Encyclopedia of Religion,* published in 2005. He has published several articles on topics related to the ancient family, gender and sexuality in the ancient world, and ideology of modern biblical scholarship, including "Contradictions of Masculinity: Ascetic Inseminators and Menstruating Men in Greco-Roman Culture."

He is currently working on issues in biblical interpretation, social history and religion in the Greco-Roman world, and sexual ethics. He has held fellowships from the National Endowment for the Humanities, the Alexander von Humboldt Foundation (Germany), the Lilly Foundation, the Fulbright Commission (USA-Denmark), and the Wabash Center for Teaching and Learning in Theology and Religion. He is a fellow of the American Academy of Arts and Sciences (elected 2009).

This chapter draws from several of our interviews and includes some additional material specific to the book.

As a historian, what can we say about Paul? Who was this man in history? What can we confidently say about him?

I should say from the beginning that you're probably going to get a bit more critical approach from me than you would get even from other Pauline scholars.

I think it's indisputable that Paul was a predominantly Greek-speaking Jew from the diaspora—that is, he grew up outside Israel or Palestine, and he comes from an urban environment. Everything I'm going on is just what we can surmise based on the kind of Greek he uses, the way he writes his letters, the things he says about himself. So I'm even hesitant to say, for example, that Paul was a Roman citizen, although it says three times in the Acts of the Apostles that he was not only a Roman citizen, but he was born a Roman citizen, which would have meant that his father was a Roman citizen.

We can't confidently claim Paul was a Roman citizen because he never calls himself a Roman citizen, or Roman in any way, in his letters, even though it probably would have been useful for him to do so when he was writing his Letter to the Romans. We can't be sure Paul was even from Tarsus, because we don't find it in his letters. There are several aspects of Paul's "biography" that we find in the Acts of the Apostles but that seem to be contradicted by his own letters. For example, according to Acts, Paul was in and around Jerusalem and Judea a lot after his so-called conversion on the road to Damascus (which is also not likely historical, when compared to his letters). But Paul insists, and insists insistently, that he was *not* in Jerusalem during that time, and that "the saints" (by which he means followers of Jesus after Jesus's death who lived in Judea) did not know him "by sight" during that time. Acts depicts Paul as always preaching to Jews in each city before going to preach to gentiles. Paul says the opposite. He insists that Cephas (Peter) was "the apostle to the circumcision," and he, Paul, was "the apostle to the uncircumcision." (This is all laid out in the first couple of chapters of his Letter to the Galatians.) If we cannot accept the historical accuracy of Acts when we have other evidence that contradicts the narrative of Acts, we shouldn't accept it even when we do not have other evidence. Paul's "biography" according to Acts is unreliable.

We have to base our historical knowledge of Paul only on his seven "undisputed letters"—those seven letters scholars generally agree were actually written by Paul (Romans, 1 and 2 Corinthians, Galatians, Philippians, 1 Thessalonians, and Philemon). From those letters we can tell that Paul was definitely Jewish. I think his predominant language was Greek. I don't think there is any evidence from his letters that he could speak Hebrew, or Aramaic, for that matter. He obviously knew an Aramaic word or phrase he could use here or there, but he could have easily picked up those in the liturgy of the primitive church.

I think Paul had at least a rhetorical education, an education in Greek rhetoric, which meant that he must have had what we would call an elementary school type, education. On top of that, he would have had the education teenage boys would have had in rhetoric: learning to write speeches, memorize speeches, and give speeches. His letters show obvious signs of that kind of education.

Paul also says that he was a Pharisee, that means from a very conservative, law-abiding, Torah-obeying Jewish family. You can't think that because he's from a Greek-speaking area, and he's very Hellenized, that means he's any less Jewish. He's very Jewish. He's also an apocalypticist. He believes that the end of the world "as we know it" is coming soon. The Messiah is going to come and create the kingdom of God on earth.

Paul is an apocalyptic, Hellenistic, conservative Pharisaic Jew who became convinced, in a surprising way, that the person Jesus, whose followers Paul was persecuting, was actually the promised Messiah of Israel. Paul seems to have been persecuting them because these Jewish followers of Jesus were allowing gentiles to join their movement without being circumcised, without "keeping" the Jewish law. But then Paul has some kind of visionary experience in which he believes Jesus appeared to him and "called" him to be "the apostle to the gentiles." (This is all, again, derived from what he says in the Letter to the Galatians, who are all gentiles.) Instead of persecuting the group of "Jesus-believers," Paul joins them. Besides believing that Jesus was the Jewish Messiah, he also believes that Jesus rose from the dead. Those are two things that, for an apocalyptic Jew, can only happen at the end of normal history. So that is where Paul finds himself: an apostle (one "sent") to gentiles to get them to accept a Jewish Messiah at the end of the current world.

He believes he's living at the end of history and he believes Jesus is going to come back very, very soon. He believes his mission: He'd been called by God, just like Jeremiah and Isaiah. When he talks, Paul never talks about his conversion. He was not converted to anything. He was called. Paul never uses the word "Christianity," he never uses the word "Christian," and he probably would have rejected both words because those would have implied that he was trying to start, what we will call, a new religion. And he's not doing that at all. He believes he's been called as a prophet by God to be an apostle. That is, one sent to convert Gentiles, to be members of Israel. They're not joining a church. They're actually being grafted like wild olive shoots into the root of Israel (to evoke Romans 9–11).

That's his mission: just like Peter was called, he believes, to get Jews to accept Jesus as the Messiah, Paul believes he was called by God to get gentiles, not only to accept Jesus as the Messiah, the Christ, but by that very action of being baptized into Jesus, they become sort of honorary Israelites. He doesn't ever call them Jews; he doesn't ever call them converts. But he also says, "some of you *were* gentiles." He talks to them as if they're no longer gentiles, because he believed they've already been grafted into the people of Israel.

In terms of dating, we're talking what, between 50 and 60 AD? He's writing about that time.

From what Paul says in Galatians, we think he must have had his vision of Christ not too long after the death of Jesus. We date the death of Jesus to about 30 AD, which is not certain but probably close enough. Now this is all guess work, but that's a lot of what historians have to do. Paul gives a timeline at the beginning of Galatians. By adding up the numbers of years he mentions, scholars believe they can "count back" and create at least a plausible chronology for Paul. We think, for instance, that he went to Jerusalem to consult with some of the apostles there after his own vision. We think Paul may have had his visionary experience as early as 34 or 35. Then his letters—or at least the ones we possess in the New Testament—were written around 50.

And these are the first documents we have on Jesus and the Jesus movement? This is the closest we have to an eyewitness?

Absolutely. Paul predates any of our other sources by twenty years or so. In fact, the only writing we have from anybody who we can ascertain to have been an eyewitness of the resurrected Jesus is Paul.

It's absolutely important for Paul to insist that what he saw is exactly the same thing that Peter saw, and the other apostles saw, because that's what he bases his apostleship on. If he just had a vision, whereas Peter actually saw some kind of physical body, Paul would reject that—because it would imply that he was a "lesser" apostle than Peter or others. And he would not accept that.

It has been claimed that there wasn't a historical Jesus, do you buy that?

I think it falls by the criterion of Ockham's razor; the rule that says the hypothesis that needs fewer and fewer suppositions added into the mix, is better than a hypothesis, or historical explanation, that needs a lot of other givens given to it. For example, Paul is the earliest example we have of anyone who claims to have seen the resurrected Jesus, but we don't believe that you can trace every early Christian document back to the influence of Paul. Mark is the earliest gospel. I would say that Mark may have known some of Paul's writings, because Paul and Mark share some theological ideas. For example, they both present the death of Jesus as an atoning death, a death for our sins. We find this doctrine in Paul and Mark, but not in Luke or Acts, which may indicate that Mark was influenced somewhat by Paul's theology. But that also shows that other early Christian documents probably were *not* influenced by Paul in any direct way.

Even just these three sources, therefore, show that we have three different historical sources, from the years around 50 to 85, that demonstrate *independent* information about details of the life and teachings of Jesus of Nazareth. Is it more plausible that they all conspired to create the existence of Jesus of Nazareth? Or that there really was a Jesus of Nazareth about whom different people told different stories? The latter hypothesis—that Jesus of Nazareth really existed, and different people told different stories about his words and deeds—is the better historical hypothesis. Otherwise, you have to invent a bunch of conspiracy theories to explain our different sources.

The best sources of evidence we have about the historical Jesus are the four Gospels that exist in our Canon, plus the Gospel of Thomas. Thomas is not in the Bible, but I would say, along with many other scholars, that it is probably one of the relatively early Gospels. Mark is the earliest, from around 70. Luke and Matthew both used Mark as a source, so they must be from, perhaps, ten years or so after Mark. So we may put Luke and Matthew in the 80s AD. Most scholars think the Gospel of John, which shows a much more developed theology and Christology, and a more developed notion of the church and its relationship to Judaism, might be dated to the 90s, or later. These are all guesses, but they are not bad guesses.

So if there's enough historical data to say Jesus existed, what, as historians, can we say about the various resurrection narratives we get from those sources?
I've written quite a lot about this in my most recent book, *Biblical Truths*, that's a book of theology. It's basically saying, I want to show you how you can be a Christian in a modern and postmodern world even knowing that a whole lot of this stuff does not stand up to the criteria of history or science. One of the things I do is I go through and point out how the resurrection accounts, the different accounts of the appearance of Jesus after his death, none of them can really meet the criteria of history. They all disagree with one another about every detail: about who saw Jesus, where they saw Jesus, when they saw Jesus, what they saw, and so on.

The earliest person who claims to have seen Jesus after his resurrection is Paul, and he claims to have seen him, probably in some kind of vision, only a few years after Jesus died. He also admits that he did not see a flesh and blood body. He says he saw a "pneumatic body," a body made of pneuma. We often translate pneuma as "spirit," but it did refer, in the ancient Greek, to a substance, like oxygen or air.

We don't know what he saw, but it wasn't Jesus's flesh and blood body, at least if we believe Paul's description of it in 1 Corinthians 15, our only eyewitness. We have one person who says he saw the resurrected body, which is historically verifiable by modern historians, and we don't know what he saw.

I find this bit so hard. What do you picture when you think about what he's claiming to have seen?
I think whatever he believed he saw, it was something that was like flashing light, because he talks about it in words that evoke that. That also matches scenes in the gospels where, in the transfiguration of Jesus, Mark talks about his clothes dazzling like lightning. A lot of scholars have argued that scene is a misplaced resurrection appearance scene. In the gospel of Mark the author has taken what was a resurrection appearance tradition that he had inherited or heard from somebody. And he puts it right smack dab in the middle of his narrative about Jesus's earthly life.

The author of Luke and Acts also speaks of the dazzling body of the resurrected Jesus. Whatever body these early Christians believed Jesus appeared in, it was assumed to be physical. But it might not be "physical" in a way we modern people consider physical. I try to say to people, imagine a body, a human body, made only of electricity and oxygen. What would that look like?

And that's kind of what they're claiming?
I think that's the closest we modern people can get to getting inside their heads. But as historians we can only suppose. We can't say what they saw. We can't say what they experienced. I think the closest we can get is saying that at least several people who had

been, or became, followers of Jesus, including Paul, really believed they saw something. They're not making it up.

But what did they see? A light flashing on a mountain side? Something mysterious at night? We don't know, but this is not too weird for history; we know there are people who believe they saw Elvis Presley decades after his death.

How many followers do you think there were immediately after Jesus's death?

I'm hesitant to speculate on this because the only time we get numbers are from the book of Acts, and those I'm sure are wildly inflated. According to Acts, the followers of Jesus meet together right after he ascends to heaven, forty days after he was resurrected. And the text of Acts numbers them as about 120.

And that seems too many to you?

To me, it seems too many to be actual committed followers of Jesus who had uprooted their lives and moved from Galilee to Jerusalem to be with him. And then stuck with him, even through his death and are still meeting in Jerusalem for months after his death.

I think it is definitely historical that Jesus appointed twelve special disciples to represent the twelve tribes of an apocalyptically reconstructed Israel. I think he also had certain women followers who were especially close, Mary Magdalene and eventually his mother, Mary. I don't think his mother was a follower of his at the beginning of his preaching ministry. But she certainly became a follower eventually. His brother, James, I think was not a follower during Jesus's lifetime. But after Jesus's death, James must have become a follower because he was the head of the church in Jerusalem after Jesus's death. We can name a few people besides the twelve disciples. It is hard for me to imagine, however, many more than say twenty or twenty-five people in the beginning.

The first documentation, as you said, is twenty years after Jesus's death. In that time Paul and others have been making converts, starting new churches; how much has the movement grown?
We know that there was no church building anywhere in the first century, from Paul all the way up until into the second century. They probably met in different houses. There were probably several house churches in Jerusalem. How many people could fit in a house church and a normal dining room? Oh, what, twenty maybe? So if you had say three or four different house churches in Corinth, would you have maybe sixty followers of Jesus in all of the city of Corinth? Would it be 120? You add Corinth with Rome, which we know had several house churches at an early period. Then we have Antioch, which was an early important center for the Christian movement. And then we have Jerusalem. And if you just go around to the separate major cities in the eastern part of the Mediterranean and then add Rome to the mix, we just have to kind of guess. Would you say by the time of Paul there may have been 500, 600? I don't know.

Who are these converts? Many are not Jews, so what is it about Paul's message, or the language of his letters that is attracting them?
One of the pioneering books approached Paul's churches that way is by my mentor and advisor Wayne Meeks. He published a book around 1983. It was a very new way of attempting to use social history, sociology, and cultural anthropology to analyze Paul's churches. He published a book called *The First Urban Christians*, and he's doing precisely that sort of thing. He's saying, what was it about Paul's message, about his theology or about the symbols he used, that would have appealed to what kind of person in an ancient Greek city?
And he tries to correlate status as people's social status, people's educational level, with images of Christianity like being a slave of

Christ, or being in a household with Christ. And he argued that there's a certain kind of a person who would have had status dissonance in his or her life. That is, maybe someone had a high education, but was not very wealthy, or maybe was a Jew but who had lots of money so could buy a bit of prestige in town. And he says, it's precisely those kinds of people that he thinks make Paul's converts and explains Paul's language.

You mentioned being a slave of Christ. Why does Paul, again and again, use slavery as a metaphor?

That's what my first book, my dissertation, which became my first book, called *Slavery as Salvation*, is about. I was trying to explain two different aspects of Paul's language about slavery, one in which he claims himself to be a slave of Christ:

Paul, a slave of Christ Jesus, called as an apostle and singled out for God's good news which He promised long ago through His prophets in the Holy Scriptures.

Why would he do that? Some people would say it's a mark of humility. And I said, no, it's clearly not a humble sounding phrase. He's boasting about being a slave of Christ. So what was it about slavery in antiquity that could have caused slavery as a metaphor to be a positive image rather than a negative image, or an image of power?

Paul also talks about himself in 1 Corinthians 9:19 as being a slave of the very people he's leading. "I have become a slave to all people to bring many to Christ." Well, what did that mean? Why would he use that language? And so I basically said that in the ancient world, it mattered less that you were a slave, than who you were a slave of. If you are a slave of Caesar, then you could be a very, very high level bureaucrat. You could be very wealthy. In fact, some of the wealthiest people in the first century around the time of Nero were imperial slaves. They were slaves of Caesar, and they ran bureaucracies. They amassed great wealth and slaves of their own and even freedpersons of their own. So being a slave of Christ would have sounded to people like being a slave of Caesar, if you have the requisite honorary feeling for Christ himself.

That explains why "slave of Christ" is actually a term of honor and power and authority. Paul uses that to establish himself as not Christ, but Christ's immediate, bureaucratic representative.

On the other hand, when Paul tells the people in his churches that he is *their* slave, "I am a slave of you all; I have become a slave of everyone," he is using a metaphor from ancient democratic politics. Advocates of the democracy of fifth-century BC Athens were called "demagogues." The word "demagogue" just comes from the Greek for "a leader of the people." It did not have a negative meaning, necessarily, except when an upper-class person such as Plato used it. These democratic politicians were arguing for democracy against more conservative Athenian politicians, who argued for monarchy or oligarchy. The advocates of the Athenian democracy called themselves "slaves of the people," just as modern politicians will sometimes insist that they are "servants of the people."

And then they would appropriate certain things, "become all things to all people," dress down, even if they were a person from the upper class. Sort of like modern American politicians. George W. Bush came from an elite background, but he tried to walk with a Texas swagger and talk with the Texas twang. Athenian politicians would try the same trick.

I identified that as a political trope and called it "the demagogue topos," or "commonplace." Paul appropriates that language in 1 Corinthians 9 to portray himself as being, admittedly, from a higher class, but lowering himself socially for the sake of "gaining" converts to Christ. All these points show that slavery, even as a metaphor, was highly complex in the ancient world.

You get stuff even before Greece and Rome, people in Egypt used to talk about being slaves of the Pharaoh, and they clearly didn't mean anything bad by it. It would sound weird today; even the

most weird and sycophantic of Trump's cabinet wouldn't call themselves slaves of the Donald.

Yes, in different cultures and societies of the ancient world, before Greece, Rome, or certainly Christianity, one finds many different ways slavery was used as a metaphor or trope. These may be similar to Greek, but not always exactly alike. In Babylonian and Persian societies, words like "slave" or also "brother" could be used by one ruler to refer to himself in writing to the ruler of another society. The words were not, of course, taken literally. They were used to create social links. And sometimes a very proud ruler could use "humble" language to refer to himself when writing to another ruler—for diplomatic purposes, of course.

In the Hebrew Bible, the word *ebed* (or sometimes transliterated as *eved* or *evid*) meant "slave" or "servant," but it could also mean something more like "assistant." In Israel, prophets are sometimes called "slaves" of Yahweh, God, in this sense. That is not at all unusual in a near eastern context. The word can have connotations of both humility (the prophet speaks not for himself, but only as a "slave" of God), but it can also carry connotations of honor (the prophet gains some social standing by being the representative of the deity).

Things change somewhat when we get to more democratically inclined Greece of the fifth century BC. The democratic politicians turn "slave of the people" into a badge of status and even honor. But that is a rather new political use of the term in a politically positive way—that is, if you are a democrat. The conservatives hated it.

Later, in Rome, you get still different uses of slave language in politics and society. This is because the very institutions of slavery are different in the Roman Republic and Empire than in earlier societies. In Rome, unlike most other ancient societies, if you are a slave of a Roman citizen, it would not be unlikely for you to be freed in your lifetime, perhaps after only about seven or ten years. And if you were freed in the normal, legal way by a Roman citizen, you became yourself a Roman citizen. You were not a "free" man, but you were a "freed" man, and a Roman. And any children you had after your own freedom—your "manumission"—were not only Roman citizens, but even "free" Romans and not just "freed" Romans. Roman freedom and citizenship were passed down through generations in ways that had not been usual in most other societies.

In Rome, something happened that had not usually happened before: slavery could be, and was, used for upward social mobility. In my early writings on slavery as a metaphor, I argued that slavery, in Paul's day and culture, could be used by at least some people as a means of social status improvement. In the end, freedom in the ancient world is just much more complex than it is for most of us in the modern world. In the ancient Roman world, there are "free" people, "freed" people, and "slaves." The children of a "freed" man, if they were born after his manumission, would end up being of higher status than their father, because they were not "freed" men, but "free" men, and Roman citizens. That explains how Paul could use slavery as a positive metaphor for believers in Christ and for himself as a "slave of Christ."

In Galatians 5:1 Paul talks about his followers being freed by Christ:
"It is for freedom that Christ has set us free. Stand firm, then, and do not let yourselves be burdened again by a yoke of slavery."
So Christ is releasing you from sin and the law, and then you're finding freedom. In other letters, Romans 6:15 for instance, he talks about Christ as a new master to whom you are enslaved. Is there a contradiction there?

There is no real contradiction in Paul's thought. It is just that slavery was complex in the ancient world, much different from modern slavery since, say, the early 1600s in the west. For one thing, slavery in the ancient world had nothing to do with "race." Slaves could and did look just like any other person, being white or brown or black or whatever. Also, slaves in the Roman world could themselves own slaves, or be the "patron" for even freedmen (who were then their "clients"). It was quite normal in ancient language sometimes to depict someone as a "slave" (say, a "slave to passions or desire") and still a free Roman citizen. Paul is using different actual social situations of slaves to illustrate different theological and relational positions of early believers. In one sense, they were free because Christ had set them free, free from sin and the powers of "this cosmos." In another sense, they had been "bought" by Christ to be his slaves. There is no contradiction, just different metaphorical uses of slavery to illustrate different theological points.

Modern notions of freedom are very much linked to individualism and an abstract notion of freedom. If you're free, you're free. I don't think Paul ever thought about freedom that way, nor, I think, did anybody else in the ancient world. Their notion of freedom was always a socially constructed, constrained one. You're only free in relationship to something else. Paul will often say "you've been freed from sin so that you can be a slave to God," or something like that.

So you're only free from a particular thing, and you're freed for something else. You're never just free in the abstract. You're free in relation to someone or something else, and Paul uses all sides of that. He doesn't say "You are freed from your slavery to sin, now you can do whatever you want." You can't do whatever you want because you're enslaved to Christ, or enslaved to God, or freed to do something good. He sometimes will put it that way; not saying "You are a slave of this," but "you are freed for this," "You are free to do this." The very notion of freedom in the ancient world doesn't mean what it has meant since the Enlightenment to the modern west. Because they always thought of everyone as so embedded, there's no such thing as pure individualism in the ancient world.

To cite another radical difference between ancient Christians and modern people: modern people, especially in the west and especially those who are not Christians, don't often like the idea that God has "foreordained" or "predestined" someone to believe in God. If we are predestined to be believers and to be saved, doesn't that mean, in modern ideology, that we aren't free? Doesn't that destroy "free will"? The ancients generally did not think that way. They tend to have thought that any person who is "free" (let's say legally) is free only to the extent of making certain decisions in certain contexts. Imagine yourself as an ant on a basketball. You are free to the extent that you can turn right or left or turn around, but you can't escape the plane of the basketball.

That's the way human beings are in Christian theology. We can't escape the being of God. We simply must live in God. We can talk about our free will and insist that we do have free will. But that doesn't mean we can do literally anything. Of course, no human being can do literally *anything*. So absolute "freedom" does not exist for any concrete being. Christians interpret that idea to say that the universe—that constrains all human beings and every being—is for us "God." God is not, in orthodox Christian theology, the same thing as "the universe," but God is the meaning that underwrites the universe. So when we say, as Christians, that we live "in" the universe, we are also saying that we live "in" God. We are constrained by the being of God. That's the way Paul thinks of freedom. Paul thinks of freedom only in a social context, you are free to be a free citizen of the body of Christ. But if you try to get out of the body of Christ, that's not an expression of freedom. You can be free only in a constrained system.

If Paul isn't using a modern notion of freedom he's still using a conception of freedom quite different from what you would get in the Old Testament, right?

You can't read Paul unfiltered from both Greek and Roman society and culture. Notions of freedom, the person, and the city, the polis have changed radically after the democracy in Athens, and other democracies. (Athens wasn't the only democracy, it's just the most famous, and the one we have most evidence for.) You can't even think of the third century BC of the Hellenistic city-states, Alexandria, Antioch, and so on, you can't even think of what notions of freedom would have been like had they not been the successors of the Athenian experiment with democracy. Freedom gets really reshaped by democratic notions, and democratic notions survive long after democracies no longer exist. There were no true democracies in Paul's day, but you can still see these traces of democratic thinking.

Remember what I said about Paul's education. He had a rhetorical Greek education. He had to learn how to give speeches in different political situation—as part of what we might call "high school." He picked up different Greek commonplaces. I don't think Paul had a fully "classical" education. I doubt he ever read Homer or Hesiod or Euripides, the main authors of classical Greek education. But when he was reading Isaiah or Jeremiah or other Jewish prophets and authors, he was reading them in Greek translation, I think always.

Remember also what I said earlier about the different political and cultural stages of the ancient world. Near eastern cultures had their own notions of slavery and freedom. Later, in the Greek democracies, things changed. Slavery was different, and freedom meant different things. When Rome takes over the Mediterranean, we have still other differences, first with the Roman Republic, and then, beginning around the time of the birth of Jesus, the Roman Empire. The Romans rejected the egalitarian ideas of democratic Athens. For that, they substituted more hierarchical ideas of the universe: everyone was supposed to occupy a steady position on a hierarchy from low to high. They also reintroduced ideas related more to monarchy: one "king" over the entire Empire. The Greek word they used (in the east) for "emperor" was actually *basileus*, the Greek word we more often translate as "king." By the time we get to the emperor Constantine and his "court theologian" Eusebius (around the years of 312–325 AD), we no longer have anything remotely like a Greek democracy or a Roman Republic. We have an empire. Notions of "freedom" and "slavery" change along with political changes.

If the language of freedom survives past its institutional expression in the form of democracies or republics, does it play a role in their reappearance centuries later? Are much later thinkers taking ideas from Greek, Roman, or Christian texts and using them to challenge the institutions of their day? That's a story that gets told.

In the grand narrative of the creation of the modern western world, which is not really my area of expertise, one would want to give attention also to the reformers, first Martin Luther and then John Calvin. We would probably also want to include the humanist thinker who agreed with them a great deal but remained a loyal Roman Catholic: Erasmus. When Luther places such emphasis in his theology on freedom, he is speaking of freedom from the law—not just "Jewish law," which is what Paul was talking about, but *any* "law" as human rules that might merit salvation. That is not what Paul meant. Calvin also, who was writing in a Geneva that was experimenting with new, modern, a bit democratic, systems of rule, also focused on individual freedom and the freedom from "works" that would merit salvation. Paul never really was talking about that, I believe. In the beginnings of the "modern west," which I certainly would place no later than the Reformation, "freedom" comes to mean often freedom from any legal requirement. It never meant that in the ancient world. And I rather doubt it has ever truly meant that in the modern world, quite literally.

What's your final evaluation of Paul's historical importance?

Paul is of course important. Some people say that without Paul we wouldn't have had Christianity. I think that is an exaggeration. Paul did not, in fact, establish the church in Rome. I don't think the apostle Peter did either, in spite of Catholic tradition to the contrary. I believe the church in Rome was founded by unnamed Jews who took the message of and about Jesus to Rome from the east and founded churches there. A lot of early followers of Jesus, who may have done the most to establish Christianity, are lost to history. We just don't know who they were.

I do think there are some things Paul did that are innovative and important for the success of his mission. One of which is that he figured out a way to bring gentiles into the church without making them fully Jewish. They didn't have to be circumcised. They didn't have to keep the Torah. I think that immediately enabled a lot of people who were drawn to the Jesus movement to be able to take it in.

Paul's other role of great importance was as an intense and focused organizer. He saw the churches he founded (and others as well, though he usually left them alone) as a network, and he worked to link them together by writing letters and visiting them several times. Jewish synagogues and Greek "clubs" did not tend to see themselves as linked together in that way. They did not tend to send emissaries and write letters to one another, trying to influence each other's behavior. And they didn't raise money together, for the most part. Paul went around raising money from all his gentile churches to support the Jewish church in Jerusalem. That was what I consider a real innovation. And it may well have been one of the most important aspects of Paul's mission that led to the eventual growth of Christianity.

That also shows that he has this vision of one church that embodies the whole world, and not as a particular ethnicity. I think Paul deserves a great deal of credit for turning what was a Jewish movement into what, potentially, could be a universal movement and then organizing it structurally with letter writing.

Do you have a sense of his personality after all of your time with his work?

People say, because I've spent so much of my life reading and publishing on Paul, if there was some person in the past that you would really like to have a beer with, I'm sure, for you, it must be Paul.

And I say, hell no! I can't imagine him as the kind of guy who has a decent sense of humor, or that you'd want to hang out with in a bar. I do find him excruciatingly fascinating because, as you know, he seems to contradict himself, he's constantly changing. I think he was brilliant, especially given the fact that we have only seven letters from him.

Further Reading

1 Corinthians
2 Corinthians
Galatians
Philemon
Philippians
Romans
1 Thessalonians
Martin, Dale. *Slavery as Salvation: The Metaphor of Slavery in Pauline Christianity*. Yale University Press 1990.
Martin, Dale. *Biblical Truths: The Meaning of Scripture in the 21st Century*. Yale University Press 2017.
Meeks, Wayne. *The First Urban Christians*. Yale University Press 2003.

3

Freedom in the Liberal Tradition

Michael Freeden

There are many, many thinkers who have influenced my political ideas and ideals; I would find it impossible to think of a single author who's developed my views the most. However when it comes specifically to methodology in political theory—how we develop an analysis of an idea, of what political arguments are, what political thinking is—I think it's fair to say that Michael Freeden has influenced me more than anyone.

Professor Freeden is Emeritus Professor of politics, University of Oxford, and Emeritus professorial fellow at Mansfield College. He is the author of over fourteen books including *The New Liberalism*; *Liberalism Divided*; *Ideologies and Political Theory*; and *The Political Theory of Political Thinking*.

In addition to his work on liberalism, Freeden is primarily known for his work studying and theorizing political ideologies. He founded and directed the Center for Political Ideologies at Oxford and is the founder-editor of the *Journal of Political Ideologies*.

He has been awarded the Isaiah Berlin Prize for Lifetime Contribution to Political studies by the UK Political Studies Association and the Medal for Science, Institute of Advanced Studies, Bologna University.

This chapter takes us through a brief history of freedom in liberalism, from the earliest liberals through to today. Specifically, this conversation explores how freedom's meaning has been debated not just between liberals and nonliberals but within liberalism, and

Michael Freeden, *Freedom in the Liberal Tradition* In: *What is Freedom?*. Edited by: Toby Buckle, Oxford University Press. © Oxford University Press 2021. DOI: 10.1093/oso/9780197572214.003.0004 how those different conceptions of freedom have radically changed the world we live in.

This conversation was recorded specifically for this volume. As the interviewer I tried to bring out both the key points in this story and highlight the way in which Freeden tells it—his focus on the contestability and constant mutation of political language.

You examine freedom as an essentially contestable concept. Can you explain what essential contestability means in the simplest terms?

There are no correct meanings of concepts. If you look at the structure of concepts, they're composed of different conceptions nestling inside each concept, and those conceptions are not always compatible with each other. You can't include all of the conceptions of a concept simultaneously. For instance, the concept of equality may include different conceptions, such as equality as identity, equality as similarity, equality of need, and equality of opportunity. As some of those are mutually incompatible, you have to select certain conceptions while the others cannot be invited in and remain as an external pile of spare parts, or alternative components. Whichever combination you have, the choice will be essentially contestable. There isn't a right one: there may be a useful one, a sensible one, an attractive one, the one that works for you, but you cannot have all the conceptions of the concept cohabiting.

The structure of any concept will always be contestable in two senses: First, it's contestable because some of the conceptions of the concept are logically incompatible with each other. You can't apply equality of need and equality of merit at the same time. Second, it will be essentially contestable due to cultural constraints. Some things are logically possible but culturally unacceptable. For instance, taking again the notion of equality, you could equalize elements in a society by simply culling either the very rich or the very poor. It's logically possible but culturally detestable. Whatever you do, you're de-contesting, which is a phrase I like to use. You're de-contesting the essential contestability of concepts, trying to end the contest by saying. "This makes more sense, this is better for this purpose, that is the conception or the combination of concepts that I like when I talk about liberty. Those I don't."

It means that concepts are constituted by flexible and shifting relationships with the other concepts with which they intersect. And if you have different conceptions inside the concept, the concepts don't exist in pure form. That happens only in the mind of some abstract political philosophers. In real-world language, concepts always bump into other concepts, interact with other concepts. Bits of one concept fall off in this clash, other bits stick on from other concepts. The components of a concept always display fluid and fluctuating patterns. So whenever you think that you're defining a concept, you're simply freeze-framing it, saying, "Okay, let's just hold it, take this snapshot," but actually the concept keeps moving all the time.

And one of the functions of ideologies is to supply meaning to concepts and link them together into a recognizable patterning?

Yes, and to decide which parts of the concept you want to include, and which cannot be included, or you don't want to include. I'll give the example of liberty here. There was a famous article by Gerald MacCallum, who had this formula:

X is free from Y to do or become Z

That is exactly what is contestable here. The anatomy or the skeleton may be identical, but it's meaningless without the flesh. The X's will change: an individual, a group, or a nation. The Y's can be the unfreedom resulting from the presence of something or from the absence of something. One can say, "I'm free from the presence of this oppressor, or "I'm free from the lack of good health that has been hindering me." And there are also crucial differences in the Z's—what happens when we are free: free to do something, to act without constraint; or free to become something, to work out my potential, to grow.

So that's roughly the bare bones of essential contestability, and the point is that contestability is *essential*. It's not temporary. It's not contingent. It cannot be otherwise. There always are debates and structural distinctions and competitions over what to include in a concept and what to exclude.

So, there's always going to be some people saying, "This is what freedom means!" and other people saying, "No, this is what freedom means!"?

That never goes away.

I reread your *Liberal Languages* collection recently. One thing that struck me, is if I went back to Herbert Spencer, or John Stuart Mill, or later thinkers like Hobson and Hobhouse, and said, "What you're really doing, when you get down to it, is you're competing over the meaning of concepts like freedom." I think many of them would go, "Yeah, that makes sense." Whereas that can be very counterintuitive for modern thinkers.

Do you think the methodology you developed is shaped by your background studying liberalism a century to a century and a half ago? Those thinkers so seem to much more self-consciously share your basic premises, or am I completely off track?

No, no, that makes sense. Obviously, I come from a liberal background, including my own family, but it's also a fascination with the flow of history. My methodology is informed by a basic assumption about the pluralism of meaning, the pluralism of language. I'm always very skeptical about truth with an uppercase T. It's wonderful for people who claim to have this truth, but I don't know whether to envy them or to pity them, because, one way or the other, they are just looking at a very particular segment of a wider possible range of positions.

It's also something to do with a tentativeness, and a modesty of research. Ideally at the end of everything that I write, I should add the sentence, "Awaiting contrary interpretation." Hence, I'm not saying "this is right"; I'm saying "this is the best I can do." I'm saying this makes sense to me, and I hope to other people as well, that's all.

In *Ideologies and Political Theory* you start with Mill as the beginning of your story of liberalism. What distinguishes Millite liberalism from those earlier liberalisms, for example Locke, such that you might not even consider them liberalisms?

As a preliminary to that, let me start by saying that the word "liberalism" began as a political term only in the 1810s–1820s. It started in Spain, then it reached the UK ten years later, usually as a very negative term. It took a while for the word "liberalism" to settle, and Mill uses it very rarely. He talks about the Liberal Party, but he almost never talks about liberalism.

It's not a political term that was common in the first half of the 19th century. That's why I think we can only talk about proto-liberalisms, because they are not part of the body of thought or ideology that we recognize from the 19th century onward as liberalism. They have the smatterings, or the antecedents, of liberal thinking. They're the seeds of liberalism, and they may be quite important, but they are not fully fledged liberal ideologies.

So back to Locke: Locke has got a notion of the protection of individual liberty as a natural right. We are born with the right to life, just as we're born with a nose. We are born with the right to liberty, just as we're born with a nose. It's just there. It's just one of your fundamental human attributes. Given that, these rights, including the right to liberty, have to be preserved, and they're preserved through what Locke calls a social contract, by which individuals empower a government to defend their natural rights when they cannot do so on their own and are in danger of being dehumanized. The other idea behind the Lockean notion of liberty is to constrain tyrannical rule, or what would at a later stage be called arbitrary rule.

Locke makes the very important distinction between liberty and license: License is the capacity to do whatever you want; but that isn't liberty. Liberty is the right to act, but under moral constraints. In other words, the notion of liberty already contains its opposite, constraint. Complete liberty is chaos. The constrained notion of liberty has to do, in Locke's case, with the respect for other people's natural rights, as well as their respecting yours. That already entails a primitive social structure, a basic community principle of mutual recognition.

What comes into liberalism by, say, Mill's day, that sets it categorically apart from that vision?

Time.

The notion that human beings are not static entities (which I think is more or less implicit in the Lockean understandings), that they undergo change, development, and maturation. Being free includes that process of development and maturation. In his famous Chapter 3 of *On Liberty*, Mill talks about the "free development of individuality." So already we have a triple, mutually reinforcing, conceptual structure: freedom, development, and individuality. You can't have one without the other two.

So we are already talking about the teasing out, and the development, of human capacities in a very important way. To be free is also to have the possibility of developing that potential, because human nature is an evolving set of characteristics, ideas, and behaviors.

Of course, there are other important things that Mill talks about. He talks about the public/private distinction, which became quite significant in the 19th century, and still is. He talks about self-regarding actions and other-regarding actions. Self-regarding actions concern only yourself and thus have no boundaries—but they are very rare. Other-regarding actions can be whatever you want only until they affect others. At that point the harm principle kicks in. So again, the notion of constraints on liberty is a very important idea.

Let me add that for Mill, there are certain features of human character that come to the fore under conditions of freedom. Originality, spontaneity, even eccentricity, in the positive sense of being interestingly different. All of these are necessary conditions of human flourishing.

Is Mill's understanding of freedom a pure negative conception, in other words simply about being left alone? The way you describe it, it sounds like there's a comprehensive moral vision of what people should be, and the moral character that he would want, that's operating alongside a defensive noninterference.

There is a comprehensive moral conception of what human beings should be, but there's no dictating on Mill's part as to what the contents of this should be. He doesn't offer any idea of what you *have* to do when you're free. It's the capacity to exercise your abilities that is important for Mill. And I think you're right; there is a sense in which Mill has preferences. When Mill says that people can do what they want in the self-regarding sphere, he might be disappointed if people degenerated or did nothing, or just lay on their backs and stared into space. Mill would hope that people themselves would be able to exercise their freedom in such a way that would be beneficial to them, and possibly also to others.

You write in *Ideologies and Political Theory*:
"Late nineteenth-century Britain is of special interest to the ideological analyst because two increasingly diverging semantic fields were competing over the denotation 'liberalism.'"
So you have two sets of claims about what liberalism is, and what freedom is, between what we might now call progressive liberalism, and libertarianism. What makes those fields divergent, particularly with respect to freedom?

One crucial distinction is that freedom is not the only concept that progressive liberals are interested in, it's rather a package. Whereas with libertarians, they tend to inflate the concept of liberty to the point where it crowds out the other concepts of rationality, of progress, of some notion of sociability, that you will find in the left- or progressive liberal ideals alongside liberty.

The first thing for the libertarian is the concentration on a roughly negative idea of liberty, to the exception of almost all the other concepts, which are far behind in the pecking order. Whereas for the advanced liberals, for the progressive liberals, liberty is crucial, but is part of a more general package. Hence Mill's trio of the "free development of individuality" are inextricably intertwined. So, that's one distinction.

The other distinction that you have, in the 19th century, is an idea that isn't competing with what I've just been talking about, but which goes off at a slightly different angle. That is liberalism or liberty as entrepreneurship, where markets, growth production, innovation, enabling individuals to make their private choices, and setting up their own criteria as to what the good economic choices are, is the valued thing.

Libertarians see us as the best judges of what is good for us, and therefore we should be allowed to make all the choices that we want, if they're not harmful to others. Whereas among the more progressive liberals, there's a very slight filtering out of some choices: irrational choices, dangerous choices, harmful choices. You can't make just any set of choices, because you're not living as a self-sustaining monad, as an atavistic individual. Whatever choices you make immediately flow out and impact on other people as well. In the more concrete sense, you're always part of an interdependent community.

So you have this liberalism as entrepreneurship, and also of course, there's an assumption here: the entrepreneurial individual is part of an unequal unit of ability. Or, in the Rockefeller version of this, there's the trickle-down theory; some of the merits and capacities of the wealthy will trickle down to others who will invariably benefit. This is based on an idea of innate inequality.

That's one semantic field. The other one is what we've been talking about earlier, which is a liberalism that is focused on removing hindrances to human flourishing. If we go back to MacCallum's "X is free from Y," The Y is now a lack. X is lamentably free from certain conditions, without which X cannot choose well, cannot flourish. X is poor, or diseased, or lacks education, and those curtail one's life-chances and ability to function. The Y is now not a human being interfering with my activities, but the burden of certain very serious socioeconomic conditions, because of which I cannot make free choices. Even if I think I'm making free choices, I'm not really making them in a deeper sense. They're heavily restricted and constrained by the disadvantages and lacks that exist in a malfunctioning society.

People often use the term "classical liberalism" quite loosely; what they seem to mean is free speech and free markets.
What you're saying is you go back to the inception of what we call classical liberalism, even if there's a loose agreement that free markets are good things, the values that underpin that are very different for these two different groups.

You realize of course, that when people use the word "classical," they're really using it in an ideological, rhetorical sense. When you label something as classical, you're saying: it's pure, it's original, it's the foundational viewpoint. It has matured in terms of its quality, and so on and so forth. Well, I'm not always sure; classical thinking can sometimes be hoary with antiquity, not necessarily in a very attractive sense. Although the word "classical" is a way of designating something as having high value: classical art, classical literature, classical Greece, I'm not quite convinced about how "classical" classical liberalism is.

But let's take this as given, we have two worldviews that are very different. One that believes in the permanence of ideas, events, and thought structures (and that is why claiming the status of "classical" is so important to them). The other believes in the continued mutation of ideas. Not only is it the case that things don't stand still, but if you think they stand still, you're just stuck in a particular past world, and not taking on board the fact that circumstances are constantly changing. Sometimes positively, sometimes unpleasantly, but they are transforming unremittingly. You have to keep your finger on the pulse of what's happening.

So good theorizing always means to build in the notion of change, of development, and of disruption as well. Which is why I prefer not to talk about liberalism but about liberalisms in the plural.

So, when you talk about developmental liberalism, or libertarianism, these are families of philosophies and worldviews, not clearly defined sets of beliefs.

Indeed. It's because our minds are so puny that we cannot grasp all the hundreds of internal distinctions that are happening all the time, and so we group them into ten, or three, or two, or one. Rather, if we look at those ideologies under a microscope we might say, "Oh gosh, there's some wonderful movement here." What we initially think we're seeing, a block of things, becomes a heaving, seething mass of changes.

How do progressive liberalism's understandings of freedom develop after Mill? For instance, how do thinkers like Hobson and Hobhouse develop the relationship between freedom and society?

Let me preface this by making the distinction between self-determination, self-development, and self-realization. Three possible things that can happen when you're exercising your freedom.

The first, self-determination is that I make my own choices, period. That is autonomy, which is simply self-government, self-rule.

Then you have self-development, which is human nature as open-ended growth, which actually can also include sociability.

And then you have the third type, which is self-realization. That can go in very different directions. It can mean emancipation in the Marxist sense, but it can also mean imposing the correct model of what it is to be human; forcing people to be free.

Hobson and Hobhouse are in the middle category here, one of self-development. Hobhouse wrote this wonderful phrase in his seminal book *Liberalism*; "Mutual aid is not less important than mutual forbearance, the theory of collective action no less fundamental than the theory of personal freedom." He twinned two ideas together, and they've become inextricable for progressive liberals. So mutual forbearance is: give me space, give other people space, give them what they want to do with it. But mutual aid is: they cannot do what they want in that space, unless there are occasions when they are helped out of their incapacity to pursue their aims when it is no fault of theirs.

That's the idea that you very often need support in order to exercise your liberty, otherwise it becomes entirely meaningless. You have, particularly in the case of Hobhouse, a notion of ethical awareness. Hobhouse was very interested in biology. He spent a lot of time in Manchester Zoo looking at the behavior of primates and trying to learn something about the human condition from them. So he was very cognizant of this notion of an evolutionary principle, and he saw liberalism as an evolutionary set of ideas, one that enhances the capacities of human beings to express themselves in a better way, and to co-relate ethically to others .

Both Hobson and Hobhouse go out of their way to say that communities are rights bearers alongside individuals. There are thus two different entities of rights bearers, and they're mutually integrated. Society has its own rights, for which it needs assistance from individuals, and individuals have their rights, for which they need assistance from the community.

Which is why the two thinkers have both attached the very important ideology of social reform to this. It's very practical, and Hobhouse is a nice illustration of someone simultaneously a philosopher and a journalist. He writes these highfalutin' books with abstract principles, but then he works as a leader writer at the *Manchester Guardian*, three nights a week. He applies these general theories to very concrete issues that arise at a particular day and in a particular week. His is a very unusual combination of a philosopher who has got his hands muddied throughout the week with the everyday job of trying to get to terms with the practical ethical issues of the day.

So you've got in Hobson and Hobhouse this idea of this mutual restraint, mutual aid, freedom requiring some degree of social support. How do those developments in progressive conceptions of freedom get us on a road that leads to welfare states?

We can see this in the Beveridge report of 1942—a plan for social justice in postwar Britain. Beveridge identified the five "giants" of want, disease, squalor, idleness, and ignorance, as hindrances to freedom. They were conditions that disable people from doing what they want with their lives—from making sensible, even if not optimal, choices.

In a way the welfare state is the coming together of this faith in the new capacity of the state. Not the state as the people who ride into your village once a year to collect taxes, or dragoon people into the armed forces, and not the state just as protection from internal or external strife. Suddenly this great organization has a new capability. It can help its members. It can empower people to do things that they simply can't do on their own. That they'd love to do on their own, but they can't.

So we have this new idea. Not the nanny state. Not the "forcing people to be free" state. But the enabling, facilitating state. It's a democratically controlled state, whose role it is to optimize opportunities for individual flourishing, without imposing forced injunctions or paths on them. And all that especially in areas where people can't provide their vital needs and pursue their life plans independently.

It's the idea that states are those organizations that have got responsibilities on their shoulders, and that they can do some good with these responsibilities. In the very early stages of welfare legislation, when the liberal government was in power in 1911, Lloyd

George talked about nine pence for four pence. The employee, the employer, and the state combined to pay nine pence for basic individual needs, but the individual only had to contribute four pence out of that nine pence. So there's added value in the role of the state.

There are downsides as well: the welfare state needs expertise, and we know in recent years how populists, or pseudo-populists, have reacted to the question of expertise as an undemocratic imposition on people's wills. Another problem is when you have a supportive welfare state but a majority decides, "We don't want a welfare state." Liberals, like any other ideology, like any other party structure, have to persuade, have to make a case for themselves, and they may fail.

If I may say this as an aside, liberals are not very good at expressing themselves in popular language. Liberals don't sing. The communists have the Internationale. The Nazis had their anthem, the Horst Wessel Lied. Liberals don't have them. Liberals are emotional, and they do feel passionately about causes like banning the death penalty, but they don't always possess the *language* of emotion—for good or bad—which turns crowds on and is a very valuable asset in politics.

So the developmental conception of freedom has been used to justify the creation of welfare states. That's not going to be uncontested however. Libertarians like Hayek won't see the increase in the size and scope of the state as promoting freedom, they'll see it as a necessary threat to it.

Yes. That's always a very difficult balancing act, because of course states are very large, powerful, and therefore possibly also dangerous (or at least uncomfortable) institutions with which to live, and the quality of a democracy is only as good as the members who constitute it. (Of course, we're living in a world where many of the major states all over the globe are increasingly behaving in very nondemocratic and authoritarian ways, and this is very worrying.)

So liberals are on the back foot. Being a liberal has always meant being under siege, to a certain extent. You can't just go forth, proclaim your liberal beliefs, and have everybody say, "How wonderful, how reasonable!" Liberals have their backs against the wall again and again and again. It's a fighting ideology, but far from the winning ideology. Even were it "winning" you have to ask, "Well, *which* liberalism is winning?" because, as I've been saying, there's more than one liberalism in town.

Hayek is a very interesting case study, because he was unaware that he was not a liberal. He has an appendix to one of his books in which he explains, unconvincingly, why he is a liberal. But his liberalism stopped in the 19th century. He insisted that the important social reforms of the liberal government before World War I were very doubtfully liberal. The welfare state is miles away from classical liberalism, or, as I would say, static liberalism.

For people like Hayek liberal principles don't require fine-tuning. Because he subscribes to the idea of a spontaneous social order, in which anything that upsets it and rocks the boat—especially state intervention—will undermine initiative and creativity. One of the determining features of conservatives is that they anchor the social order in extra-social forces removed from the human ability to control them; God, the "laws" of economics, history, nature, biology. The spontaneous social order is yet another motif on the same theme.

Which persists with us today, admittedly often in a much less sophisticated form, when people just proclaim the laws of the free market, or the laws of economics, almost as they might invoke natural rights; as something freestanding and obvious.
Would that be the heart of your case for why libertarianism isn't liberal; that it seems to share this core conservative premise?

Yes, and because it is unreflective. When you identify a law with a capital L, it's very comforting. "Oh yeah, we're just not going to worry our little heads about it. That's how the world works." That is a deeply, deeply culturally conservative idea. Liberalism, and to some extent Marxism as well as various forms of socialism, all get their energy from challenging received truths. In a way, this is what people like myself employed by universities are paid to do. Our job is not to teach this or that course, but to question received truths and only then to recommend accepting or rejecting them or, even better, to leave that choice to our students.

Attlee wins, and we do the NHS. FDR wins, we do the New Deal. That's followed by a period in which, although some of them might have opposed it at the time, the main political actors and parties seem to broadly accept that these things are here to stay. This gets called the postwar consensus. Then falls apart with the Reagan and Thatcher revolutions. Why?

Well first of all, before why it fell apart, why was it the consensus? It was the consensus because all might agree on the creation of the welfare state, but we always need to examine the small print. For conservatives the welfare state meant greater productivity and greater social stability, whereas for the left it would mean greater social justice, equalization, and the capacity for human develop-ment. So under the macro-banner "welfare state" you get com-pletely different micro-ideological positions.

So why does it break down? Well partly it breaks down because people realized a consensus had never existed in the first place: all that had happened was that the hairline fissures simply overlapped a bit more, and partly because we are living in a period in which the grand ideologies have been questioned, at least in reasonably open societies.

I think what has happened was that the obsession with grand solutions began to disintegrate. The Keynesian model, which was supposed to be foolproof, began to break up in the 1960s and '70s, accompanied by the recognition that the world no longer harbors just a two-superpower system in the international arena, but hosts a multiplicity of medium to strong powers.

Partly what occurred was that the postwar consensus succumbed to the notion that ideas and positions change very rapidly. We are living after all in the 21st century, where technology changes at such a speed that it's not surprising that the social constructs around those technologies also mutate with considerable rapidity, and do so all the time.

We are also continuously revamping our understanding of what democracy is, with digital electronic platforming of this, that, and the other. No sooner have you laid something down than it erodes within a few years. Whereas even in the first part of the 20th century, you were living with these grand systems of fascism, communism, democracy, or capitalism. The world seemed relatively simple, and then it turned out to be not so simple. The human race has been living, what, some quarter of a million years on this planet. Yet the past 100 years have gone, in terms of tempo, out of control. It's a miracle that we as human beings can keep our mental and cultural stability under such conditions of transformation, and many don't, even at a societal level.

Unsurprisingly, these notions of consensus can only be constructed by highly abstract political philosophers such as John Rawls, who refined a particular American constitutional model, thinking, "This will work wonderfully for the rest of the world," which itself is a form of cultural arrogance. Rawls himself was a very modest man, but he adopted a notion of prescriptive uniformity. It is a formula for a world of justice, but it does not embrace the multiple ideas of justice among different cultures. It is a parochial view—emanating from North American academics— masquerading as a universal one.

This is not a liberal prescription. It's not a liberal approach. One cannot impose a "correct," or singular, decontextualized liberalism.

Since you mentioned Rawls. We started with a seeming consensus that fell apart: "classical" liberals agreed on free markets, but they

agreed on them for very different reasons, and as time and events move on that consensus falls apart.

Then after the Second World War, people across the spectrum agree on the welfare state, but they agree on it for different reasons, and that consensus falls apart.

What do these stories tell us about the possibility of achieving a final agreement in politics. A permanent, overlapping consensus, as Rawls would have it?

I don't believe in a permanent overlapping consensus. I know that I wouldn't want one.

In order to arrive at the notion of an overlapping consensus, you have to thin out the consensus very, very severely. I mean, you can say, "Okay, there are certain constitutional principles we can agree on," but then many people will not like those constitutional principles, and for good reasons. Not just for egoistic or nationalistic reasons, but because some of the constitutional principles are hidebound. They're very difficult to change. They may freeze the wrong formula. Even a thin consensus is biased toward values one may wish to question later on—think of shattered views on gender, race, or sexuality that were once unquestioned.

The word "permanent" frightens me, and I wouldn't like to live in a world of "consensus." So that leaves the word "overlapping." Overlapping is fine, but let's just recall that the overlap is fleeting and transient. It inevitably keeps changing, and needs to change, incessantly.

The things that overlap in 2010 may not overlap in 2015, and may not overlap in 2020. Think on how our assumptions about the world have been modified over the past decade. Of course, we want to arrive at some overlapping conversations, otherwise we can't understand each other. But the idea of a permanent overlap would be stultifying, and it would close off future options. It would mean the end not only of politics, but of human creativity.

It would also be impossible. Language behaves in its own way, and human thinking behaves in its own way. It doesn't need permanence, it'll never achieve permanence, and it shouldn't achieve permanence.

Further Reading

Freeden, Michael. *Ideologies and Political Theory: A Conceptual Approach.* Oxford University Press 1996.

Freeden, Michael. *Liberal Languages: Ideological Imaginations and Twentieth-Century Progressive Thought.* Princeton University Press 2004.

Freeden, Michael. *Liberalism: A Very Short Introduction.* Oxford University Press 2015.

PART II
PHILOSOPHY

4

Feminism and Freedom

Nancy Hirschmann

What are the most important things to say about human nature? This question, which recurs again and again in this volume, is tied closely to how we understand freedom. Should we assume that people are individuals who make their own choices, who want to be left alone, and are best served by doing so? Most of us would say yes; the question then becomes, is there anything else we would want to add, any other considerations that should inform how we treat people?

In this conversation Nancy Hirschmann makes the case that individual choice—while undoubtedly important—is not sufficient, that we must also understand the context in which choices take place. Far from being a purely theoretical debate, it is of great consequence for how freedom is distributed in the world. Specifically, she describes how thinking of freedom 'just' as individual choice can blind us to the lack of freedom many historically disenfranchised groups, such as women, face.

We start the interview by covering what philosophers call positive and negative liberty. The distinction between the two, and the debates surrounding them, are key to much of the work done in the field on freedom. Hirschmann outlines factors, such as material circumstances, ideology, and social construction, that she argues must also inform into our thinking on freedom and gives some concrete examples of this. I end by asking her what a feminist conception of freedom would look like.

Nancy Hirschmann, *Feminism and Freedom* In: *What is Freedom?*. Edited by: Toby Buckle, Oxford University Press. © Oxford University Press 2021. DOI: 10.1093/oso/9780197572214.003.0005

Nancy Hirschmann is professor of politics at the University of Pennsylvania one of the world's leading experts on the philosophical foundations of freedom. In her seminal *The Subject of Liberty: Toward a Feminist Theory of Freedom*, she undertook a detailed analysis of the concept, and how it might apply to difficult social issues such as Islamic veiling and domestic violence. She has also written on freedom's history, in *Gender, Class, and Freedom in Modern Political Theory*. Hirschmann considers how the development of our dominant conceptions of liberty were impacted by class and gender. More recently she has worked on disability and freedom—how disability, and language evoking disability, has set a limiting condition on freedom in the history of political thought that is still reflected in today's political theory.

This interview was recorded specifically for this volume, and some additional material was added through email exchanges between me and Professor Hirschmann. I learned a great deal through the process and sharpened my understanding of some key philosophical terms. I hope readers do too.

There's a tradition of philosophers talking about positive and negative liberty or freedom. In the simplest possible terms, what do people mean by that distinction?

Isaiah Berlin is credited with creating this typology, and he first says negative liberty is an absence of barriers, restraints, or obstacles, much like Hobbes. But this apparently simple definition becomes more complex quite quickly, for Berlin goes further, introducing intentionality and agency; somebody has to cause the obstacle. That's his focus in his famous "Two Concepts of Liberty" article. Then, in "From Hope and Fear Set Free," he goes further again, defining freedom in terms of "open doors," arguing that the more options you have to choose from, the freer you are. Those two ideas are connected in the sense that if a door is open, presumably no one is blocking your way.

Yet he says this rather curious thing, which is that the more doors I have open to me, *even if I can't go through some of them*, the freer I am. He indicates that negative freedom entails the presence of opportunities that may be irrelevant to the material, concrete conditions of your particular life. For instance, I may not be able to purchase an item of clothing because I am poor. Berlin says those things may affect my "ability" to do X, but not my "freedom," as long as the door is open and nobody is purposely preventing me from going through it. In contrast to someone like Gerald Cohen, Berlin rejects the idea that large-scale social forces like poverty are obstacles to freedom per se.

That's one problem that I see with Berlin's formulation. I believe that large social forces can be obstacles to freedom, and denials of that idea are what makes systemic restrictions placed on large numbers of people invisible.

In the United States the term "systemic racism" has entered the mainstream as something that entails the limitation of the freedom of persons of color in myriad ways more than of white persons. And feminists have long talked about "patriarchy" and sexism as structures that restrict women. Now, these large systems in many cases result in individual identifiable actions, such as police using a chokehold or a boss firing an employee for not sleeping with him, but there are also much broader and less identifiable ways that these systems constrain the freedom of many groups of people.

And positive liberty?
Positive liberty is even more complex in terms of the multiplicity of versions that people have come up with. Berlin thought of positive liberty as totalitarian mind control. In his view a totalitarian state tells you, "The state is vital to who you are, and therefore the good of the state is really what you want, whether you realize that or not." As a Russian Jew who lived through the 1917 revolution, he's worried about the Soviet Union and Stalinism, and he sees a tradition in political philosophy that led to it, particularly Rousseau's *forcer d'etre libre* (forced to be free). But I think that we have to reject this view as simplistic.

Instead, I think there are three "layers" to positive liberty. One involves the provision of the resources that you need in order to take advantage of negative liberties: for instance, scholarships for education if you cannot afford tuition; or a wheelchair if you have lost the use of your legs in an accident. These resources enable you to pursue things you want, such as getting a degree, or mobility. The second layer is offered by Charles Taylor's "What's Wrong with Negative Liberty," namely the notion of internal barriers, the psychological and emotional conditions that impede us from following our desires. Taylor argues that we can have conflicts about our desires and even desires about desires, which he calls higher order desires. For instance, I might have decided to quit smoking, but a stressful event makes me crave a cigarette. I go outside and light up. Am I actually doing what I want? If a friend snatches the cigarette from my lips, she is arguably helping me to do what I had previously decided is my true preference, to quit; in a sense, she is taking away my choice in order to maximize my choice, that is, to help me free myself from my habit. That's what Taylor calls the second-guessing problem: if we start complicating what desire is, and acknowledge both that people can have lots of different conflicting desires all at once, and that people have the capacity to evaluate the importance of their desires, then we have to allow that other people can intercede on our behalf. Because often, other people can see us more clearly than we can see ourselves. Obviously, that has to be navigated carefully, so this second layer of positive liberty is fraught with difficulties and Berlin was right to be concerned about it.

But it leads to the third layer. What Berlin ignored, and Taylor hinted at but never consciously took up, is something that Foucault brings us to, namely the understanding of how those desires get formed and perceived in the first place. Why it is that I have certain desires and not others, and rank some desires as higher or more important than others? How did I come to be the person that I am with the desires that I have? How are my choices, which continue to define who I am, shaped by the social context in which I live? As I asked in *The Subject of Liberty*, how does my subjectivity, my identity as the desiring subject, get constructed by history, by custom, by the culture I live in, such that I want the things that I want? Foucault helped us see that every person is constituted by forces that conglomerate over the course of history. That means that the assumption that lies at the root of negative liberty, that the individual is completely self-forming, is false. Instead, we are inherently social creatures. So rather than looking just at what I want, we also have to look at the social context for the desires we have and how the obstacles to those desires came into being. Why do certain obstacles exist to certain desires and why do certain people feel certain desires and not other desires?

So the phenomenon of desire, and where it comes from, how we feel it, recognize it, identify it, and express it, is extremely complex and variable. That makes it difficult to say freedom is doing what I want to do without restraint. Doing what I want may be necessary, but it is hardly sufficient; indeed, sometimes doing what I want will paradoxically reduce my freedom. So freedom also has to involve an analysis of why I want something, the conditions that have informed that desire, the conditions in which the desire would be enacted, and what the consequences of that enactment would be.

Do you think the positive-negative divide is even the most useful typology in the first place?

It depends what you think the typology is really about. I don't think it offers us two concepts of freedom per se, but rather two conceptions of what it means to be a person. If freedom is really as essential to humanity as the Enlightenment theorists say it is, then freedom has to start with our understanding of who we are as human beings. And each model captures aspects of our humanity that the other ignores. In negative liberty, we are choice-making, independent individuals. In positive liberty, we are deeply social, historically situated, and emotionally and psychologically multilayered. So both models provide an extremely useful language for capturing certain aspects of our humanity.

That's sort of what I'm driving at though, is that the distinction, if it's useful, it's, like you say, between two conceptions of human nature (which obviously relate to freedom). But if you go back and you look at the history of political thought, most people don't easily categorize as one or the other.

Right.

So if I'm teaching a class on freedom and I say, okay, you can basically put everyone in one of these two boxes, that's not a useful way to think about it.

That's correct. In my book *Gender, Class, and Freedom in Modern Political Theory*, I showed how Hobbes, Locke, Rousseau, Kant, and Mill, who tend to be categorized as one or the other, in fact all deploy both conceptualizations at the same time. Now, we could conclude this means the typology is useless. But instead I think the typology provides us with a conceptual terminology for understanding these different components of human experience that are in conflict with one another, and within individuals themselves, as they are expressed in these theories.

I've been a critic of negative liberty, not that I don't think it's important, but I don't think its sufficient. Also, I don't buy the argument that if we include anything else in our conception of freedom that way madness and political authoritarianism lies.
I think you would agree, so let me ask you this: what do you think is the strongest argument for an exclusive focus on negative liberty?

Nobody likes being told what to do.

Yeah.

Or more precisely, we all want to feel like we are exerting some control over our lives; even animal studies show that the lack of such control has strongly deleterious effects. There are some who would say that that is a specifically western idea, but I would venture to say it's fairly universal at this point in history; many see democracy movements in China and the Middle East as movements for liberty, for instance. It may be more extreme in the West—the refusal of some Americans to wear masks in the name of freedom is a particularly stark, if not absurd, example.

That all makes total sense. My pushback, and I think yours too, is against the idea that anything outside of that will end in the Soviet Union.
I agree, that is an incoherent position based on a fantasy. "Having control over our lives" cannot simply be reduced to "being left alone." Instead, it requires lots of structural support, support that many of us, particularly people with privilege, just don't see. Extreme negative libertarians ignore the way they got to the position that they occupy and the lives that they live. But all of us are shaped by our social structures every day. Many of us benefit from social structures that make our choices possible, but we fail to recognize them as enabling conditions, we just think that's the way things are. That makes it easier to adhere to strict negative liberty and ignore the systematic and structural ways that some have been enabled to make those choices while others face obstacles that we don't recognize.

You've mentioned social construction. Can we break that down?
Sure.

I'll play the antagonist. I could say to you, "Yes, I recognize that there's society and whatever, but I get up in the morning and I chose to eat a crumpet and not a waffle. I really did that. There

was no society whispering in my ear telling me what to do. That's really at the core of who I am and as a person!"

The desire for good-tasting food may be naturally hard-wired, and food has cultural and emotional significance. But the specific choice of a crumpet is shaped by the specific culture and time you live in and the options that are afforded to you. That choice, and its internalization into your identity, is already historically and culturally situated in ways that we would need to pull apart.

I've argued that there are three different layers to the idea of social construction. The first is ideology, which often entails a false misrepresentation of material reality. For instance, consider the patri-, archal belief that women are irrational, and they therefore shouldn't be educated. Feminists from Mary Astell to Mary Wollstonecraft to today have said that's false. It's a "social construction" as if the idea of "construction" is at odds with truth. It refers to a set of beliefs that's evolved over time, developed over time, that is at least an overgeneralization and often downright false.

But there's a second layer, which I call materialization. As Wollstonecraft argued, if you think women are irrational and you deny them education on the basis of that, you are going to produce women who don't learn how to think rationally. Boys don't spring from the womb capable of rational thought, it's something that they are taught. So the ideological belief makes itself true through the way it structures material relations. The third layer is what we might call discourse. The first two layers depend on an assumption that there's this "Truth" out there with a capital "T:" women are in fact rational, and if you would just stop oppressing them their natural rationality would emerge. The third layer is more complicated and pertains to language. If patriarchal ideology about women's irrationality materializes into the exclusion of women from education, thereby producing women who are more interested in flirtation than philosophy or science, then we develop a concept of femininity that is very much tied with sentimentality, with emotion. We're going to think that a woman who wants to go to university is unfeminine, because that's for men. That is, ideology, and the material practices and institutions that support it, produce an entire conceptual structure and linguistic formation about what is it to be a woman or a man, so that we no longer see the ideology per se but only a naturalization of what we've created. So discourse operates at a very deep level that we're not even aware of. These three levels of social constructivism are interactive. It's a constant process of going between ideology, materialization, and discourse, and it affects every aspect of our identities and therefore shapes freedom: not only the options that are available to us, but our very desires. To return to Wollstonecraft, if I learn from childhood that my purpose and sole goal in life is to catch a husband and have children, she asks, how can I even imagine myself as an educated professional?

To apply that to my silly case of eating a crumpet, say I've been told to be healthy, but also happen to find crumpets tasty when they have lots of butter on them. That ideological conditioning might well affect how I perceive that choice, which desire I give priority, how I respond to authority, how much credence I give medical expertise, or diet advice.

Yes, that's right. Whether I accept my doctor's orders would depend on a lot of different things—including my economic status, which may affect my ability to purchase the foods my doctor recommends, as well as my and the doctor's gender and race and the relationship of trust or mistrust that develops because of those factors. Additionally, there are more individual factors, such as you note: my attitudes toward authority, my trust of medicine, which often changes its recommendations about what is good and bad for us, and of course the important emotional work that eating certain foods does in my life. All of those individual aspects are as social as my race, gender, and economic situation, and they will affect my choices even though I'm not consciously aware of many of them.

When you look at it for the small choices it seems obvious to the point of being mundane; clearly I'm influenced by the people around me and the culture I live in. But the more you think about it the more it seems to have to power to overwhelm everything. Someone might ask "if it's all just constructed, does the idea of any sort of objective truth just fall out altogether?"

That has been the primary objection to the third layer of social construction, associated loosely with "postmodernism." It constitutes what I call the paradox of social construction: if everything really is socially constructed, then it does seem that there is no objective reality or even the capacity to say, for instance, that patriarchy is worse than feminism, that racial equality is better than racism. How do we make value judgments about different kinds of institutions? And are we socially constructed to make those judgments? That's why I argue for seeing social construction in three layers; because ideology is "real" even if it's "false," and it produces material practices and institutions that are real and that produce their own truth.

For "real" and "true" are distinct ideas, even if they are closely related, and I think that the idea of "truth" as something that is universal, transhistorical, and beyond lived reality has been seriously problematized by this kind of framework. That doesn't mean that facts don't exist: the earth does rotate around the sun. But the truth claims that philosophers are concerned with—such as freedom or justice or human nature—are much more uncertain. I distinguish between "real" and "true" because for me, social constructivism doesn't lead to any particular conclusion about how we should live our lives. Instead, it provides us with a framework for being more self-aware of the choices that we make, and for thinking more about why we do things and what it is that we really want.

Can you talk us through some concrete instances of how choices might be conditioned by material circumstance or ideology or culture or convention?

In my earlier example, an ideology that women are irrational and intellectually inferior leads to a material practice of barring women from university, thereby ensuring that women will not become learned or skilled in various professions. That will lead women to "choose" what they are in fact coerced toward, namely marriage and motherhood: ideology produces a self-fulfilling material reality. This may or may not be what women "really" want, but they have never been in a position to ask themselves that question. In the 1950s Betty Friedan called the dissatisfaction of many American housewives "the problem that has no name" because imagining a set of social relations where women were equally valued as men, and could share in both paid work and in childcare and household responsibilities equally with men, was just inconceivable; and yet women were extremely dissatisfied with their choices but saw no alternative.

Change started with resistance: rejecting this ideology produced demands for changes in material conditions. So-called consciousness-raising groups and protest movements were more about saying what women were dissatisfied with at first, and it was only later that positive demands began to be formed, and alternative futures imagined, as the idea of what it meant to be a woman changed. That imagining and struggle is continuing today in ways that early feminists of the 1960s couldn't have imagined. But that's because the changes in the social construction of the meaning of "woman" and "feminine" made it possible to imagine other previously unimaginable meanings. So desires and choices change as subjectivity changes, and subjectivity changes as the social and discursive practices in which people live change. It's an interactive dynamic.

Now consider that after all these changes, the majority of household labor and childcare in heterosexual marriage is still done by women, for a variety of reasons, including persistent ideological and discursive beliefs about what it means to be a woman and a mother. But there are also material reasons; they may have stopped working or switched to part-time work when they had children because their husbands had higher salaries, as is often the case. And men have those higher salaries because of various ways in which sexism operates in the marketplace, thus in effect overdetermining women's choices to "opt out."

Women's choices have not been coerced in the negative liberty sense, yet their desires have been formed through social relations that have at their core a system of male privilege: men are paid more for the same work, they are rewarded more and punished less if they "help out" in the home, and so forth. And of course women are socially expected to be the primary caretakers, it is once again tied up with the notion of what "femininity" means, and many women internalize those pressures. All of these factors cannot be abstracted out of women's apparent "choices." They are ideological, material, and discursive.

Changing these kinds of social constructs is extremely difficult because often they are difficult even to see and identify. But consider what's happened in Sweden, where there has long been extremely generous parental leave compared to most other countries. Though parents were free to divide up this leave, women took the vast majority of it and men took hardly any, often because of professional pressure. Sweden changed that by requiring that a certain portion of the allowed leave had to be used by the father or the couple would lose those months. So fathers started taking it, and there is now even cultural pressure on men who do not take it to do so.

As a result, men's attitudes about child care and their place in the family are changing; the ideology of feminism has produced a material condition that is changing how people think about what they want and the choices that they make about how they divide up household labor.

It's an example of social construction that operates in all three layers but in the opposite direction of my education example. You start with the same patriarchal ideology saying that women should care for children. But then feminists challenge that ideology, offer their own counterideology of gender equality, and fight to change laws and policies to create new material relations. These have created changes in the discourse about masculinity and femininity; and this in turn should produce opportunities for new and different choices, not just in terms of the options available but in how we can imagine our futures.

Could you use that case from Sweden as a counterpoint to Berlin's concern about authoritarianism?
You still respect choices in the negative sense—at no point do you tell people to have or not have children, or even who should do child care. It's just in addition we're considering material circumstances, institutions, and ideology.

Yes, this policy isn't coercive because men are not forced to take it; but it's creating an opportunity structure that creates social pressure on men to take it: carrots rather than sticks. Of course extreme conservatives, who like to think of themselves as negative libertarians as long as you don't try to bring about significant changes like having men participate in childcare, might think this is still social engineering and therefore unacceptably authoritarian.

But you haven't interfered with negative liberty, in that case that you just outlined.

That's right. But for many people, anything that threatens the status quo, particularly in matters of gender and race, is seen as authoritarian, dangerous, or radical. Such people can never be appeased because they simply want the world the way they want it, and anyone who disagrees with that is going to be labeled either a radical or a social engineer or a Stalinist. These people generally believe they are defending negative liberty ideals because they want to preserve choice for themselves, but they actually represent the very nightmare of authoritarian positive liberty that Berlin feared: a world where only certain kinds of choices are seen as consistent with freedom, a world where only certain kinds of people actually get to choose. Much of corporate America is headed by people with these attitudes, and the U.S. has terrible parental leave.

That brings me to the last aspect of social construction, namely power. The paradox of social construction that I mentioned earlier could be taken to suggest that freedom is a relativist ideal: it might seem that one social construction is as good as another, patriarchy as good as feminism, and so my conception of freedom doesn't allow me to criticize the extreme conservative. He's just advocating for a particular construction of social relations. But the material relations of power mean that some people are better positioned than others to influence the institutions, practices, and structures that socially construct us. In the west, for instance, white people have more say than people of color in shaping laws, workplaces, criminal justice systems, all of which have material effects on the lives we live and the ways that we see ourselves: 'systemic' or 'structural' racism. And throughout the world men have more power than women in these areas—which I have called "structural sexism"— just as wealthier people have more than poor people under capitalism. Although nobody ultimately controls how we are socially constructed, and all of us participate in it in some way and to some degree by the choices that we make in living our daily lives, some people are structurally positioned to have more power to influence it than do others.

How do you sum that up into a conception of liberty? A quality that negative liberty has is I can put it in a sentence. I can say something like the absence of deliberate interpersonal constraints. Do you have a sentence to sum up your vision?

Well, I hope I have successfully made the case that any simple definition of negative liberty cannot be sustained, but rather opens up a range of questions about what we mean by choice, desire, restraint, barrier, and so forth, requiring us to bring in issues that pertain to positive liberty.

But if I had to sum up my view of liberty it would be something like this: Freedom is about the ability to make choices about how we live our lives, and to act on them; but choice must be understood and evaluated both in terms of the material conditions in which it is made and the internal conditions of identity and self-conception that give rise to desire.

Negative liberty's emphasis on external barriers is an important starting point to my conception. But at the same time, the definition of what constitutes an external barrier needs to be enlarged beyond what most negative libertarians allow. We must consider the productive forces of the "external" environment on the "internal" self, desire, and will, borrowing from positive liberty's notion of internal barriers and the social construction of the subject. Combining both positive and negative liberty elements in the idea of what constitutes a barrier means that the line between internal and external cannot be clearly drawn; rather the two must be seen as mutually constitutive.

Similarly, to make the idea of "choice" truly meaningful entails the material provision of a much wider array of meaningful options and opportunities that are genuinely available than is the case in many societies for many groups of people, such as women, people of color, and less affluent persons. This requires equality in two senses. The first is equal access to resources, in keeping with that first understanding of positive liberty I mentioned earlier. But even more important is equal participation in the processes of social construction. I say "processes" because I consider social construction as ongoing, a function of relationships in language and time; and I say "participate in" because nobody has the kind of conscious control over the creation of the self or others implied by the term "construction," even though some structurally have more power and influence as I have just said.

In practical terms, this would require equality in social relations ranging from the sexual division of labor in the family to the creation of law and public policy, but social construction is also importantly about the normative framework in which we live and understand our daily lives. It is my belief—and perhaps this is what makes some people consider me a liberal despite all of my talk of social constructivism—that changing norms will come from changing the people who occupy positions of power. Such change will, perhaps paradoxically, help weaken, if not undermine, structural inequalities of sex, race, and class. And I believe that it will create greater freedom for all.

Further Reading

Berlin, Isaiah. "Two Concepts of Liberty: An Inaugural Lecture Delivered before the University of Oxford on 31 October 1958," in *Four Essays on Liberty*, 118–72. Oxford University Press 1958.

Berlin, Isaiah. "From Hope and Fear Set Free." *Proceedings of the Aristotelian Society* 64, no. 1 (June 1, 1964): 1–30.

Hirschmann, Nancy. *The Subject of Liberty: Toward a Feminist Theory of Freedom*. Princeton University Press 2002.

Hirschmann, Nancy. *Gender, Class, and Freedom in Modern Political Theory*. Princeton University Press 2017.

Taylor, Charles. "What's Wrong with Negative Liberty?" First published in *The Idea of Freedom: Essays in Honour of Isaiah Berlin*, ed. Alan Ryan, 175–93. Oxford University Press 1979.

5

The Liberty Principle

John Skorupski

John Stuart Mill is referenced multiple times in this volume; indeed, it would be difficult to imagine a collection on freedom in which he was not. I've spent a lot of time with Mill personally—I usually reread *On Liberty* once every year or so. While everyone should read the original—its importance to the history of freedom is hard to overstate—it can be helpful to have an expert guide you through Mill's thought whether you're encountering it for the first time, or revisiting it.

In my humble opinion, the best scholar to serve as guide is John Skorupski. His short book *Why Read Mill Today* is the best introduction out there for a general reader. In the early days of the podcast I had the pleasure of discussing with him one of Mill's most famous formulations—the liberty principle.

John Skorupski is the Professor Emeritus of Moral Philosophy at St Andrews University. He studied Philosophy and Economics at Cambridge University. After lecturing at the University of Glasgow he moved to the Chair of Philosophy at Sheffield University in 1984, and to the Chair of Moral Philosophy at St Andrews in 1990. His interests at the moment are: moral and political philosophy, meta-ethics and epistemology, and history of 19th- and 20th-century philosophy.

Professor Skorupski's books on moral and political philosophy include *Symbol and Theory: A Philosophical Study of Theories of Religion in Social Anthropology, John Stuart Mill, English-Language Philosophy 1750–1945, Cambridge Companions to Philosophy: John*

John Skorupski, *The Liberty Principle* In: *What is Freedom?*. Edited by: Toby Buckle, Oxford University Press. © Oxford University Press 2021. DOI: 10.1093/oso/9780197572214.003.0006

Stuart Mill (edited by John Skorupski), *Ethical Explorations*, and *Why Read Mill Today?* His upcoming work *Being and Freedom: On Late Modern Ethics in Europe*, covers freedom extensively, looking at the concept in France and Germany, as well as the United Kingdom.

You wrote a book titled *Why Read Mill Today?* This seems like a reasonable question to start with, who is Mill and why might we want to read him today?

John Stuart Mill was a 19th-century philosopher and political activist. He was born in 1806. He died in 1873. He served in parliament for some years in the 1860s. According to himself in his autobiography his biggest contribution was that he almost got women the vote in the 1860s, which is impressive because they didn't fully get the vote until seventy or so years later.

He also had a very interesting childhood; he was the son of a man called James Mill who was an associate of Jeremy Bentham, the great utilitarian. They had theories about educating children, which he tried out on his son. He got a kind of turbo boosted education, Greek at the age of three, that kind of thing. He felt afterward sad and wistful about what he'd missed as a child. That's a famous part of his autobiography, which is a very short book and regarded as one of the classics of the 19th century. So, philosopher and political activist, with a famous background, perhaps that sums it up.

The single idea Mill is most associated with is the liberty principle. What is that in the simplest terms?

The problem of course is putting it in the simplest terms. The way Mill approaches it is that he gives you a whole variety of formulations, which have puzzled people ever since. Then he has a whole book expanding and qualifying it. The simplest version that people usually use is that the liberty principle, which they often call the harm principle, is the principle that we shouldn't stop people from doing anything they feel like doing, unless it's liable to harm others:

the sole end for which mankind are warranted, individually or collectively, in interfering with the liberty of action of any of their number, is self-protection. That the only purpose for which power can be rightfully exercised over any member of a civilised community, against his will, is to prevent harm to others. His own good, either physical or moral, is not a sufficient warrant. He cannot rightfully be compelled to do or forbear because it will be better for him to do so, because it will make him happier, because, in the opinions of others, to do so would be wise, or even right.

But then, like you say, although that's the simplest account of the principle, it's actually somewhat misleading because the question just becomes, what do you mean by harm?

Exactly. When we go down that route, that can go on forever. Mill was writing for an intelligent public; lots of people bought the book. Nowadays, we do philosophy academically and we try to define terms, and the word "harm" turns out to be very difficult to define. Once you've defined it, it turns out not to do all the things that Mill wanted to do with the liberty principle, and so you're in trouble. I'll give you an example: take the question of whether people can be compelled to act on juries. Are you harming anybody if you refuse to act on a jury?

What he says is, "look, I've explained to you this principle up to a point, but now I want to make some further explanations of what it involves." So, for example, I'm not trying to rule out the idea that people have certain obligations to society such as serving on a jury if asked to do so. He doesn't say that they're harming anybody if they don't. That would be stretching it a little bit; who do I harm exactly by my personal decision not to act on a jury? So what he says is no, there are certain basic political obligations that we can insist people have. And he bases that not on the idea of harm but on the idea that you're acting unfairly if you opt out.

Another limitation is that the liberty principle, according to Mill, only applies in reasonably advanced nation-states. It only kicks in at a certain point in society's development.

Yes. Society has to reach a stage where "people are capable of being improved by free and equal discussion." Prior to that, people could only hope for a benevolent dictator; "there is nothing for them but implicit obedience to an Akbar or a Charlemagne."

So if harm is something of a misnomer, because it just sort of pushes the philosophical can down the road, could you think of another way of summarizing the general normative thrust of *On Liberty*?

Well, as I say, Mill actually proceeds by, first of all, giving you a whole variety of formulations at the very beginning, of which the harm version is one. What he's trying to do is to get you to see it from a variety of angles to get a grip on what the intention is—as opposed to a formula that you apply like a lawyer.

But I think that you capture the most important aspects with a sort of inelegant, or disjunctive, formulation. I think harm is one of them. Obviously, if your action is going to harm others, it may be appropriate to stop it. I think a second thing is the one I've just been talking about that you may be compelled to do certain minimal obligations to society, you know, like appearing on a jury, on grounds of fairness. And a third one, which has caused an awful lot of controversy (and in my opinion misunderstanding) is that you may be asked to refrain from behavior that's bad manners in public, that intrudes, as one might put it, on others in a shared public space.

But excluding "offenses against decency," excluding the demands the state can put on you to maintain itself, and excluding duties of assistance toward others, he wants to carve out a very deep "private" space for individual's own plans, their own ways of life?

Oh yes, absolutely. He's "exhibit A" as far as that kind of liberalism is concerned.

Can you draw a distinction between Mill and contemporary philosophical liberalism, such as John Rawls, that this is not an abstract set of rules? This is not the idea that the state should be neutral. It's all very much based on a conception of the human good and human flourishing.

Both parts of what you said are true. He tries to base the liberty principle on something like the principle of utility. That is, on what's best for human beings considered impartially. Also, chapter 3 of the essay *On Liberty* has this very eloquent defense of the idea that what's really good for you is your self-development, not development by others; you should develop yourself in the way that's best for you:

> He who chooses his plan for himself, employs all his faculties. He must use observation to see, reasoning and judgment to foresee, activity to gather materials for decision, discrimination to decide, and when he has decided, firmness and self-control to hold to his deliberate decision. And these qualities he requires and exercises exactly in proportion as the part of his conduct which he determines according to his own judgment and feelings is a large one. It is possible that he might be guided in some good path, and kept out of harm's way, without any of these things. But what will be his comparative worth as a human being? It really is of importance, not only what men do, but also what manner of men they are that do it.

Now we could discuss whether that's not a bit hopeful and unrealistic, when we're talking about everyone, down to the biggest couch potato, and not just people with outstanding qualities of self-determination—but it's definitely his view.

Is this a purely individualist account?

He's a utilitarian. Utilitarians are impartial individualists. They think that everybody counts equally and nothing counts ultimately other than the well-being of individuals. So they're individualists in that sense. They're not theorists of self-interest, they're not against cooperation. They're not libertarians who think all that matters is rights. Their ultimate criterion is what contributes to the well-being of human individuals, considering all human individuals equally.

So, this is a much richer notion of human flourishing and social cooperation than simple rights protection?

Yeah, actually my own view about "philosophical liberalism," at least as it developed in the 19th century (which is when it fits best), is that it should be characterized by what we've just been talking about: the idea of self-development. The philosophical liberal of the 19th century thought that the real case for liberty is ultimately that it helps people to develop themselves, and that it brings them closer to well-being. That's true of Schiller, and it's true of Humboldt. Mill actually picked up a lot from German liberals—he was following in their footsteps.

Mill gives a very vivid account of self-development as an organic, natural process (in contrast to the "mechanical"). Why did he use this evocative language?

The short answer is that he was appealing to the spirit of the age. Also, bear in mind that Bentham's utilitarianism was treated by many people like Thomas Carlyle (who was in some sense a friend of Mill's) with great contempt as a mechanical, dusty, sawmill. Mill felt that he needed to distance the basic philosophical idea of utilitarianism from this stereotype of mechanical thinking. That made him a great admirer of Coleridge. He saw Bentham and Coleridge as the two half-men of their age: You had to combine what was right in Bentham with what was right in Coleridge, and get rid of what was wrong in each of them. And Coleridge was very into organic metaphors for personality and society.

So one argument for freedom is letting people lead their own life in their own way leads to self-development. The other is that freedom helps advance society. Mill talks about "experiments in living" as an example of the latter, what does he have in mind here?

He actually doesn't say what particular experiments of living he has in mind. I would guess, if you asked him, he'd come up with small-scale socialist experiments, because they're the ones that he clearly took a great interest in. He wrote about socialism and was very interested in the idea of approaching it experimentally. Not taking over the country and making it a socialist country, but allowing free scope for those kinds of experiments of living: communes, cooperatives, going off and living a green life as against an urban life. Seeing how well they would do and what they could teach.

There's no reason you couldn't apply it to other examples though. For instance, I don't think Mill had much idea of, say, the power of today's religious cults and prophets, but, strictly speaking, he would have to say, "yeah, that's another example," so long as it respects the liberty principle. Billy Graham is giving you an experiment in living. You see whether you like it or not.

So, Today he might be interested in the occupy movement, or the people who go off and try to start a nature commune. What about groups centered on psychedelic drug use? They often invoke the liberty principle.

Yeah, absolutely he might have been interested in nature communes. I was simply guessing at the kind of things that he would have had in mind when he wrote. Probably he would steer clear of drug experiments, but his view on drugs would have to be that they could only be criminalized if taking drugs causes harm to other people.

Does it follow from this argument that we should let people take whatever drugs they want?

And degrade themselves so long as they weren't harming other people? I'm afraid so, yes. That's precisely the sort of thing that other liberals later in the 19th century picked Mill up on. They wanted to introduce, for example, restrictions on drink. They wanted to introduce those restrictions precisely because they thought that liberalism requires you to stop people from degrading themselves. And that is a line of argument that you could get from the basic premise of philosophical liberalism: If the big thing is that you should be trying to improve yourself, develop yourself, why shouldn't we help you by stopping you from taking drugs and drink? That's a line of argument which people put against Mill, but he was definitely not going to give way to it.

I think there's two responses. One is the negative effects of criminalization (locking people up for instance) outweigh its benefits. The other is there may be positive aspects to drug use: some people have done experiments that do seem to show psychological, or even normative, benefits from psychoactive drug use. I'm not sure how you weight potential gains from one elite thinker against one hundred regular degraded users though.

You've just put a really cogent question to John Stuart Mill, and the sad fact is that he never considered it. In other words, supposing that some of these elitist experiments of living do show us a new way to live, but at the cost of causing harm to other people who think they can follow it, but just end up degraded druggies. What is your trade-off? That's a question that Mill doesn't answer, but a relevant point would be that he doesn't think an activity can be stopped any time it is going to harm other people. The liberty principle puts a necessary, not sufficient, condition on interference. Mill comes up with plenty of examples of things that harm other people where it's not okay to stop them. If you and I take part in a competitive examination, where there's only one person required for the job, you're harming me because you're going to get the job by taking part in the examination. Nobody's going to stop you for that reason.

So, what if this experiment in living by Dr. Joe Bloggs, who's really into unusual esoteric drugs, turns out to give extraordinary mental experiences to the few, but drives many other people into just being addicts who get no self-development out of it at all? If that's the situation, then I think Mill would be committed to saying, well, it's a trade-off and I've got to consider how much harm is caused and how much elevation of the human personality is caused. It's a very good modern question, we've had lots of experience of this.

The liberty principle isn't just a prohibition on state interference in self-regarding action, it's also a prohibition on social interference. What's meant by the latter?

The principle limits moral constraint, as well as legal constraint. For example, you might think that adultery is wrong but that it shouldn't be illegal. Does Mill want his liberty principle to cover these nonlegal moral constraints? Yes he does. He wants it to cover them because he's very keen on the idea that there's a power of mass conformism in modern society which operates independently of the law, and you've got to do something to oppose it.

Take the case of gay relationships, Mill would go further than saying they should be legal; he would also say we shouldn't judge or create any sort of social pressure?

I think in the case of homosexuality, he would not be neutral but would judge that it is not morally wrong. Nothing is morally wrong unless it harms others or it violates one of the other two things I mentioned. But homosexuals are not taking advantage of others' contributions, like someone who refuses to appear on juries. If they act in a way that intrudes on others in a public space, that is objectionable—but exactly the same applies to heterosexuals, right?

Would that apply to all nonconventional relationships? Polygamy or polyamory for instance, that not only can we not criminalize, we can't even judge?

You can judge them as being morally permissible. The liberty principle is meant to work as a criterion of when moral condemnation is legitimate—and when it is not.

I want to emphasize however that Mill's attitude has a Victorian forcefulness. He would come up to you and say "you're saying other people's sexuality is wrong, you are wrong!" He wouldn't say "well that's your opinion, but let's leave out the morality of it because I just want to decriminalize it." He wants to change moral opinions.

If you're wrong it's my obligation to point that out to you. Your opinion, if it becomes too common in society, is going to harm people in a way that's unacceptable. It's going to infringe on their liberty, simply because conformist moral opinion can have an oppressive power. I've got to stand up against it.

Mill's moral forcefulness also comes out in another way. He thinks that important areas we usually think can be left up to individuals have to be policed by moral opinion or law. So he thinks that people should not have children if they are unable or unwilling to look after them. Procreation in such circumstances is greatly harmful to the child.

It is also the parents' responsibility to make sure that the child is properly educated. Where the parents are financially unable to do that, the state should pay. But if they have the funds yet fail to make sure their child is properly educated, they should be fined. So Mill's understanding of liberty is not very close to that of people nowadays who think of themselves as libertarians.

It is interesting to see how most of his detailed discussion of examples still goes to the heart of present-day debate. He still serves, for some, as a moral compass, and for others, at least as a point of reference.

Further Reading

Mill, John Stuart. *Autobiography*.

Mill, John Stuart. *On Liberty*.

Skorupski, John. *The Cambridge Companion to Mill*. Cambridge University Press 1998.

Skorupski, John. *Why Read Mill Today?* Routledge 2006.

6

Freedom as Nondomination

Phillip Pettit

One of the most important intellectual movements concerning freedom in the last fifty years or so has been the re-emergence of republicanism as an active political philosophy.

Republicanism has always been a tradition in the history of political thought, but until recently it has received comparatively little attention. This started to change with the writing of "civic humanists" such as Hannah Arendt in the fifties and sixties and Pocock in the seventies and eighties. These thinkers argued that the goods of active political participation and civic virtue are intrinsically valuable components of human flourishing.

More recently an alternate interpretation of this tradition emerged, starting with Quentin Skinner and Phillip Pettit, that centered the theory on a "neo-Roman" conception of liberty. According to Skinner and Pettit, participation and virtue should be understood as an instrumentally useful tool for securing political liberty. Liberty, according to these theorists, is being removed from arbitrary rule, or "domination."

From this central starting point, the two thinkers developed distinct, though compatible, intellectual projects. Skinner worked on the historical origins of this understanding of freedom (as well as on historical methodology), looking back to thinkers like Machiavelli, as well as lesser known figures.

Pettit, while also interested in history, used this conception of freedom as a starting point to develop a more comprehensive vision of the good society. What does freedom, according to this

Phillip Pettit, *Freedom as Nondomination* In: *What is Freedom?*. Edited by: Toby Buckle, Oxford University Press. © Oxford University Press 2021. DOI: 10.1093/oso/9780197572214.003.0007 conception, imply for our political and economic institutions? How should it affect how we see the purpose of law? Pettit's intellectual project has built, from a central ideal of freedom of nondomination, a total worldview of morality, politics, and society. Indeed, he goes so far as to argue that, as far as politics is concerned, freedom as nondomination is the only good we need worry about, so expansive are its implications.

Philip Pettit is L. S. Rockefeller University Professor of Politics and Human Values at Princeton University, where he has taught political theory and philosophy since 2002, and for a period that began in 2012–2013 holds a joint position as Distinguished University Professor of Philosophy at the Australian National University, Canberra. He was appointed a Companion of the Order of Australia in 2017. Born and raised in Ireland, he was a lecturer in University College, Dublin; a Research Fellow at Trinity Hall, Cambridge; and Professor of Philosophy at the University of Bradford, before moving in 1983 to the Research School of Social Sciences, Australian National University; there he held a professorial position jointly in Social and Political Theory and Philosophy until 2002.

He was elected fellow of the American Academy of Arts and Sciences in 2009, honorary member of the Royal Irish Academy in 2010, and Corresponding Fellow of the British Academy in 2013; he has long been a fellow of the Australian academies in Humanities and Social Sciences. He holds honorary professorships in Philosophy at Sydney University and Queen's University, Belfast, and has been awarded honorary degrees by the National University of Ireland (Dublin); the University of Crete; Lund University; Université de Montreal; Queen's University, Belfast; and the University of Athens.

This conversation guides the reader through an overview of the modern republican project. It starts with a question of ethical foundations: Should our politics be aimed at delivering a good or at following rights? We consider what both approaches entail, and Professor

Pettit argues for a "goods-based" approach. From this the question naturally arises, which good (or goods) should the state concern itself with? This leads us to the substance of the discussion: a republican conception of freedom as nondomination. We look at the history of this ideal, what it means, and how it might contrast with other conceptions of freedom. Finally, we discuss a range of applications including freedom in the workplace, antitrust regulations, the market, and the relationship between freedom and law.

Robert Nozick famously starts *State, Anarchy, Utopia* with the claim: "Individuals have rights, and there are things no person or group may do to them (without violating their rights)."
By "rights" he means a system of individual property rights which serve as his ultimate ethical justification. How would you assess that as the foundation of a political theory?

He believes in what are often called natural rights. These are supposed to be rights that you can just see. They happen to be justified. They are the basic currency of moral thinking.

I don't think that it makes much sense to imagine that there are rights that are "just there" from nature or something. Rather, it makes sense to think that there are things that we naturally, as human beings, find good or valuable, satisfying or appealing, as social creatures. I think that the rights that we give one another should be determined by the goods that are thereby produced.

Rights really are just the other side of the coin to rules; wherever you've got rules, you've got rights. So, if you just take the rules of chess, they give you the right to move the bishop on the diagonal, but they don't give you the right to move it in any other way. Wherever you've got rules governing human behavior, you're going to have a right. What is a right in that sense? It's something that others have got to allow you to do so long as we're going along with those rules. So, if you're playing chess with me and you say, "I don't want you to move the bishop on the diagonal," I have a right against you and you have an obligation to me, given that we're playing under those rules. Whenever you have rules, they confer, or establish rights (and also of course obligations, like I'm obliged to allow you to move your bishop on the diagonal).

I think that someone like Nozick fetishizes rights. He takes right away from any context of rules and says "they're just rights! These are our natural rights!" This is an example of what I call the "Cheshire Cat fallacy" (Remember in *Alice in Wonderland* the Cheshire Cat is that cat that disappears, but the grin remains). The Cheshire Cat fallacy, as I think about it with rights is the fallacy of thinking that you can remove all rules, and still find rights remaining; the sort of rights that rules would establish. We all understand what it is for there to be rights given that they're rules, but these people are saying you can pull away the rules and the rights will still remain in place. Then they call them "natural rights" or "fundamental rights" meaning there are no rules that support them. There are no rules that are on the other side of those rights.

This isn't a matter of being on the left or the right of politics, this is a matter of pure philosophy. I just think it's very bad methodology. It offends against parsimony, the principle that you should not introduce unnecessary entities into a theory, to think, "oh, I'm going to postulate natural rights." We already understand that certain things are good, that they appeal to human beings, and that in order to achieve those goods, human beings set up rules. In order to enjoy the good that comes from a parlor game they set up rules like the rules governing chess, and when they have the rules, they have rights within them. More generally in society we establish rules that prevent violence, that establish order, and possibilities of exchange between people. As soon as you have rules like that, whether they're informal norms or formal laws, you've got rights that are the other side of those rules.

It seems to me, though, that most people are really resistant to that way of looking at the world. Even professional philosophers, or people who've really thought about it. They really want to hang on to some set of deontic constraints and I'm not really sure why. Do you have any thoughts on that?

I think I do: If you have a set of absolute deontic constraints as you call them, like rights for example, or duties on the other side, that are not based on rules and not based ultimately in the good those rules do, that gives you a sort of clarity. It might be mysterious in the sense of where on earth do these rights come from, but it gives you rules to live by that are absolute. You don't have to justify them or see the good they do in order to live by them; you just say, "this is the rule." It's the appeal of the Ten Commandments, it's the appeal of any guidelines that are just laid down. The idea is that it's not our part to ask about whether they're good guidelines; that's not your business. You should just follow the guidelines.

It actually comes from a tradition, I think, of religious thinking which says, "God tells us what to do, it's our part to do what he says, to follow the rules that have been laid down," and not to ask about whether or not in a given case more good might be brought about by breaking the rule. There's an old Latin tag that goes back at least a thousand years to capture this idea; *fiat justitia ruat caelum* (let justice be done though the heavens may fall). The idea is God looks after the heavens; God will look after the consequences of following the rules, your part is just to blindly follow.

Very few people take that view nowadays I hasten to add, but I think that's the genealogy, the origin, of the idea, and the appeal of these deontic rules. It sort of exonerates you of responsibility to think about the point of the rules.

So, in your progression of questions for a moral or political theory we just dealt with the first question: A goods-based or rights-based approach. The next question is what is the good that we should design our states to promote?

There are many different responses of course: One traditional response was, and I suppose this is still true of religious societies, that the state should be promoting the good according to some received religion.

The utilitarian tradition that emerged in the 1800s with Bentham, that you've cited, said, "well let's just boil it all down; isn't it all just about human happiness and welfare, can't we all agree on that?" I think there's something to be said for that sort of theory, but it's not a theory I invoke myself.

What I'm inclined to say is let's go back to a value everyone prizes, everybody says is important, and that's freedom. I think we should think of the main good that the state is there to establish is the good of freedom.

Of course, there's then immediately a question of what you mean by freedom. For me the traditional conception of freedom that was in place down to the late 18th century is a conception that we should be retrieving. This is the conception that was, for example, endorsed by the founding fathers in America and has a tradition that goes right back to Rome. I think that notion of freedom gives us a very plausible account of the good that states should be pursuing.

When you say "going back to Rome" you're referencing what is often termed a republican theory of freedom?
Yes.

What is the republican theory of freedom and how might it contrast with a libertarian or "neoliberal" theory of freedom?
In order to introduce this what I often do (in a recent book, Just Freedom, I use this a lot) is take the case of a woman like Nora in that wonderful play by Henrik Ibsen; A Doll's House. She's married to Torvald, who's a young banker. Under the law of the period, and in Ibsen's play, Torvald has all the legal power. He has the power to dictate what she wears, who she associates with, if she can go out on her own, whether she can go to the theater, whether she's got a choice in religion, and so on. He has total power over her finances

and how much money she has to spend obviously. Torvald dotes on Nora; absolutely dotes on her. He gives her carte blanche; she can act exactly as she wishes, within the normal range of choices.

A question I often ask in trying to deduce these ideas is, do we think that Nora is free?

There is one way of thinking about freedom, the common way I would say among libertarians, which is to say that all freedom means in a choice is that no one gets in your way. You're not interfered with; no one stops you, no one penalizes you, no one threatens you with penalties, no one deceives you, no one manipulates you. If no one in that broad sense interferes then you're perfectly free in a choice. If you take that way of viewing freedom, you'd have to say that Nora enjoys an enormous amount of freedom. She enjoys freedom as noninterference, as I like to call it.

I remember presenting this in a lecture to a very large group in China some years back. I asked about five hundred undergraduates, "is Nora free?" They all chorused "NO!"

Ask yourself: why isn't Nora free? It doesn't take much thought to realize that Nora is not free because, while she can act as she wills, she can only do that so long as Torvald is willing to let her act according to her own will. It's his will that is ultimately in charge. When she goes to the theater, when she wears what she wants, she's enjoying a latitude of choice, but she only enjoys it by virtue of his permission.

This points us toward another way of thinking about freedom, which I think really was the dominant way of thinking about freedom right down to the late 1700s. In this way of thinking about freedom in order to be free, it's not enough that you're not interfered with, it must also be the case that there's no one who's got the power of interfering with you at will. You're going to be unfree to the extent some other person can determine whether or not you can act as you wish within the realm of relevant choices. I call that "freedom as nondomination."

The Romans were very, very clear about this: take a slave whose master allows him or her to act exactly as the slave wishes, is the slave free? The resounding answer in Roman thinking is that no, the slave is not free; the slave is not a *liber* (a free person). The slave remains a slave. Even with a kindly, sweet, goodly, easily deceived, gullible master, she still has a master. She's under the will of another person, even though that person allows her, so to speak, to act exactly as she wishes.

For the Romans, and for the long tradition down to the 1700s, to be free meant you had to have the status of no one being master over you. They used the Latin word *dominatio* to describe what a slave suffered in relation to a *dominus*, or master. So, I (and lots of people nowadays) call that way of thinking about freedom "freedom as nondomination."

So, the antonym in each case is different? The opposite of freedom, according to a libertarian, is interference. Whereas the opposite of freedom, according to a republican view, is domination?

Exactly. Now that has two really important implications: one is we should worry about arrangements under which one person has power over another, even if the person who has the power is relatively benevolent or benign. That's socially quite radical: that each person should have some sphere in which they are master in his or her own life. They should have some range of choices where, except when they want it to be so, there is no one who stands over them.

The other implication is how you think about the state; it always interferes with people in laying down the law, and applying the law, but if it's controlled appropriately, democratically, and with constitutional constraints, it doesn't interfere with us just according to its will. It interferes with us according to terms that we share, the terms that should be imposed on government, so that government, while it interferes, does not dominate. Freedom as nondomination condemns domination even where there's no interference. Just like

Torvald, it says you just shouldn't have those sorts of arrangements. But it's prepared to be accepting of the need for a state that interferes, provided that state is not dominating.

So, a logical consequence of freedom as nondomination is that it necessitates a democratic element in power arrangements. It necessitates a participatory element of any sort of state apparatus because, if you are subject to interference, to be free that interference cannot be arbitrary, so must (in some sense) be authorized by the community it's being exercised over.

Or in some way at least controlled by the community. I think of the control we have as "we the people" establish terms, in common deliberation which we come to take for granted. We concretize them in our institutions. What we require of government is that it be disciplined, that it acts, as I put in the title of one of my books, *On the People's Terms.*

That certainly, I think, requires electoral democracy. It also requires constitutional constraints on government that are established and unbreakable, short of there being a constitutional amendment. It also requires a system in which people are enabled to contest government, at every point. I think there's a huge range, and that's what democratic theory should be about. Determining what are the best instruments whereby you can contain government, and ensure that, while we allow it to interfere (that's the condition you pay for having laws and social order), we require it to be constrained, on our terms, in how it interferes.

For example, I said that in the private case the benevolent master (or husband like Torvald) is an enemy of freedom, even though he's benevolent. Equally the government, no matter how benevolent it is, is an enemy of freedom if it's unconstrained, uncontrolled, undisciplined, not subject to the people's terms. It's in fact a benevolent despot.

You can think of republicanism as being opposed to benevolent mastery (or mastery of any kind) whether in private life or in public life. It's despotism, no matter how benevolent, because the will of the person with power, private or public, is the will that's in charge. That means that your freedom is already compromised, even if there's no actual interference.

Does that theory apply to power structures which affect our lives other than states or governments? For instance big corporations like Amazon or Facebook.

Well my answer is yes! I'm afraid our world is replete with forms of domination which, in a properly regulated legal system, would be seriously contained.

You mentioned Facebook, I wrote an article called "The Big Brotherhood" looking at the big social media providers. I argue that the problem isn't just that they have access to private data, the problem is that by having access to it they're in a position to exercise all sorts of power over us. To that extent it's not just an assault on privacy, it's an assault on freedom. So, it's ironic in a way, that something designed to encourage free speech should actually become a system in which our freedom goes with our privacy. The privacy is breached by bodies that have power, it's not as if it's a peeping Tom or someone intruding on your life who has no power over you, that's just a breach of privacy. If the person has access to data on you that they can use to blackmail you, or persuade you, or get in under the radar to manipulate you—even if they don't use it—they've got power over you. Even if they don't use the power, the fact that they have the power means they dominate you.

That's a contemporary example, but there are so many other examples of domination. You mentioned corporations, one thing that really worries me is the rapidly evolving (I would say degenerating) state of workplace relationships in corporate life. One thing that really worries me is the right of an employer, this is particularly important for corporations, to fire at will, which exists in American law.

So, what does that mean? It means that an employee is at the mercy of the manager who can fire or hire at will, just at his wish. Given that being fired always has serious costs (even if you can get another job there are transaction costs as well as immense psychological and social costs) it means that there's someone there who's got this power of interfering in your life that's unregulated.

I would argue very strongly that in any employment situation it ought to be the case, at least for employees who've been there a certain time, that there should be a procedure that has to be gone through if a manager is going to fire you. The procedure need not be all that demanding, but it should put some cost on the manager so if he or she fails to fire someone, it's embarrassing. Then there's a bit of a constraint. The manager doesn't have the same dominating power.

In employment relations, again in the United States, unions have almost disappeared. Unions have not been an unalloyed good, but neither have corporations, and when they were both there they constrained and contained one another. With unions gone employees are now basically exposed to the whims of corporate power—and boy has that power been exercised!

For example, not only is there a right to fire at will but nowadays there are a lot of employment relations that involve a noncompete clause. This means that if you voluntarily leave the corporation you can't work for the same industry for a certain period of time. That means that you're tied to that industry. It means that, again, you're dominated. You don't have the freedom to change job in effect, because you've got this hanging over you.

Recent legislation has also made it very difficult for employees in America to bring a class action lawsuit against a corporation because of so-called arbitration clauses in the contracts that say that in the event of a complaint you go to an arbitration panel. You can't go to a court with people from the same industry or working for the same corporation. It's an immense loss of power.

Employees have lost an extraordinary amount of power in America in the last quarter of a century or so. There is real domination in the workplace to that extent, even if employers are highly benevolent.

One of the things that I see both in my day-to-day life, and in the comments I get from the podcast, is people who, by the liber-tarian standard of freedom are free, do not feel free. People who have middle-income jobs, have the freedom in theory to leave those jobs, they're not being constrained or interfered with in any way. But they feel trapped in their jobs because they wouldn't be able to support their families without them, hence they're not in a position to refuse an instruction that they find unethical or humiliating.

So, you have this contradiction of people who are materially as prosperous as anyone in human history has ever been, who are, according to the socially dominant definition, free but in a pro-found way don't feel free. I'd be interested in your thoughts be-cause I think that's such a common experience.

That is a matter of great concern. In order to enjoy republican freedom, law would have to establish what used to be called the basic liberties. That is to say a set of choices such that everyone, in that range of choice, is sovereign: they are their own master.

For people to have an area of choice where they were (in that sense) free would require a law that protects them against unem-ployment by providing dole, that guards them against serious ill-ness by making medical insurance available, and guards them against being brought before the courts when they don't have the resources to defend themselves.

Now if you had a society in which people didn't have this fear, where they were their own men and women, they might form re-lations where they become dependent on one another, but they would do so voluntarily, from a position of strength.

On that image of society people can walk tall. There's a long tra-dition in republican writing, particularly in 17th- and 18th-century England and America, of talking about freedom as the ability to walk tall, not having to bend the knee, not having to kowtow, not having to tug the forelock, not having to live under the thumb of anyone else. It's associated with a sort of forthrightness and frankness.

John Milton, writing about the English republic, talks about how in our republic people will be able to walk with their heads held high. I call this the "eyeball test of freedom"; in a society where people really did have freedom as nondomination in the range of the basic liberties equal with others, they would be able to look each other in the eye without reason for fear or favor. That seems to me a nice image of the ideal for the freedom we're talking about.

Notice though, that's taking feelings as the most powerful index of whether you're free. That you can look others in the eye without feeling fear. (Or rather without reason for feeling fear; you might be highly timid and with all the protection in the world would still feel fear, that's your problem. If the society is well organized, you at least don't have a reason for fear.)

If people are feeling trapped in their jobs there are of course natural circumstances we're all hemmed in by. An economy that's flagging for example, means that fewer jobs are available. But assuming you're working in a society where the economy is growing at a reasonable rate there is no reason that people should feel trapped like that. If they do, it may be because of the problems in employment relations that I talked about: The problems of being able to be fired at will, the problems of having signed up to not work in the same industry, these are the sorts of issues that undermine that feeling of freedom.

There could be a set of abstract rules that say you are free (for instance, you're not being interfered with, you have the theoretic freedom to choose your employer) but at the end of the day how much does that set of abstract rules matter? Aren't concrete institutions important too?

We're talking about various rules, for instance laws governing workplace relations and so on. But those rules are an aspect of the institutions that we should have. In addition, there ought to be a law allowing unions to form. But just having the law wouldn't be enough: you'd also have to have people willing to form unions for example, and you'd have to have people willing to back one another up so that individuals don't feel alone. They feel like others have their back or are in the same situation.

These are institutions that the state can't manufacture. We have to rely on civil society to construct those. It's a comment on our civil society that often it doesn't deliver those sorts of protections. Move from the case of workers to the case of women: it's one thing having a law against domestic abuse, it's another thing having a community in which you'll be backed up if your husband (which is usually the case) is abusing you. Or to have a backup network of women who will help a woman in distress, provide housing and so on. It's very important we have those sorts of civil society institutions as well as the formal laws. All of this is part of having a society that enables people and empowers them to enjoy this freedom as nondomination. Law is really crucial, but it's not enough on its own.

What are your views on the role of law in antitrust? How would you feel about a law that simply did not allow corporations to gain more than, say, 60% market share? That would be a direct violation of a libertarian conception of freedom, but it might be required by a republican one.

Yes, it would be, and here you find an area in which I think the political right and left might find some common ground. After all, the antitrust legislation in America in 1910 comes from a recognition that it's one thing to have a free market in which people can make contracts of all kinds, it's another to have a market that produces appropriate goods. When you have monopolies those goods get compromised.

That's true also of the good of freedom as nondomination. The marketplace can actually be a great force for freedom as nondomination, for example, Adam Smith arguably shared this view. The argument is that the great thing about the free market is you're not tied to a particular master; you can move on to another master. He said the subject of many masters is the subject of no master; as you can always go and find another master. So, from the very beginning the notion of the free market has been associated with freedom as nondomination.

I would say, in the longer tradition certainly, it's been recognized that the market will not deliver that good under various circumstances. One of them is when you get monopolies established then there's nobody else you can go to work for if you specialize in the area of the monopolist. Further the consumer dealing with the monopolist is at the mercy of the prices he or she sets without constraint.

So, it's always been recognized really. Those who say, "just let the market rip because that's what natural rights require," are really very ahistorical. The Market grew up around ideas about the good that it could produce and the need to regulate it and constrain it in various ways (like the antitrust legislation) in order to ensure that it produces these goods.

The justifications and philosophy that surrounded market systems when they came into existence was so much richer, so much better in many ways, than the very narrow justifications that we get for the market nowadays. Some people seem to have this almost religious deference: we just have to do what "the market" says. We just have to follow that set of outcomes regardless. The only limit worth the name is that of noninterference.
Whereas, the initial vision of the market of Adam Smith, or a little bit later the idea of perfect competition, or a Walrasian Equilibrium, is a model of many buyers, many sellers, perfect information, no barriers to entry.

The interesting thing, just to take corporations first of all, Smith himself was highly critical of corporations. Although there were few in existence at the time, he was highly critical of them. He saw them as congealing power in a few hands, basically to the detriment of most people. He was certainly in favor of the much more decentralized market you're talking about.

Now our markets are controlled more and more by corporations. These bodies are given more and more power by the laws of different countries. They have the power for instance to threaten countries to go offshore so that the country will actually defer to them and make laws that suit them: say, to loosen up workplace relations, or axe environmental regulations. It's an extraordinary amount of power. It's totally antithetical to the original vision.

There is a way, and I would like to mention this, that some economists (maybe right-wing economists I guess) often delude themselves about the agency and power of corporations. They say that the corporation is itself a market, and imply that it cannot therefore act like an agent to a dominating effect, which is really a serious mistake. The corporation certainly involves people tied to one another under their individual contracts, as people are contractually tied to one another in a market. But it is a group of people organized to act for the corporate goal, not an impersonal arrangement like the market in which there are individual agents but no group agent.

You could say that of a nation-state. You could say that of anything. On one level it's true enough, if banal, that everything is "just" individuals. The question is what are the power structures in which those individuals exist, and to what degree can they be compelled to act in conformity with a shared set of goals?

Well, you're singing to the choir! Music to my ears, I entirely agree with that! We have to recognize that corporations, like states, are institutional agents in their own right. That they've got enormous power and by having power they can dominate individuals, both the people who work for them, their consumers, and now, more and more, the very states in which they operate. They've become so powerful relative to states that they play states off against one another in a race to the bottom. All of that means that they're enjoying the sort of domination that is absolutely inimical to the freedom of ordinary people.

Could we say though that there is a zero-sum conflict between republican liberty and libertarian liberty (as understood in a contemporary sense) but that the solution isn't that the republic defeats the market, the solution is a restoration of the original vision of markets? A restoration of seeing them as one tool among many that can, in specific circumstances where power is more diffuse, be a vehicle of freedom as nondomination?

Yes. I certainly agree with that.

Maybe one theme on which to end is this: The two ways of thinking about freedom are interesting in the following respect. If you want freedom as noninterference, you must hold that all laws interfere, so they take from your freedom. The implication is you should be really, really wary about having too many laws or regulations. You just let people go their way without laws, except for the very basic laws needed for nonviolence and whatever. You recommend a night-watchman state. Law is the enemy of freedom, except in that minimal manner.

If you go with freedom as nondomination, you must recognize that freedom depends on the law. Law defines the sphere of basic liberties in which you can enjoy freedom as nondomination. Law gives you the protections, in virtue of which you can stand tall and enjoy the exercise of freedom as nondomination in the sphere of the basic liberties.

So, on the one hand the libertarian way contrasts freedom with law whereas a republican sees freedom as requiring law. That means you've got to really massage the law and get the law right, the law governing corporations, governing marriage, governing democratic institutions, and so on, in order for people to enjoy freedom within the law.

Further Reading

Lovett, Frank. "Domination: A Preliminary Analysis." *The Monist* 84 (2001): 98–112.

Pettit, Philip. "The Freedom of the City: A Republican Ideal," in *The Good Polity*, eds. Alan Hamlin and Philip Pettit, 141–68. Blackwell Publishers 1989.

Pettit, Phillip. *Rules, Reasons and Norms*. Oxford University Press 2002.

Pettit, Philip. "Freedom in the Market." *Politics, Philosophy, and Economics* 5 (2006): 131–49.

Pettit, Phillip. *On the People's Terms: A Republican Theory and Model of Democracy*. Cambridge University Press 2012.

Pettit, Philip. *Just Freedom: A Moral Compass for a Complex World*. W.W. Norton & Company 2014.

Skinner, Quentin. "Machiavelli on the Maintenance of Liberty." *Politics* 18 (1983): 3–15.

Skinner, Quentin. *Liberty before Liberalism*. Canto Classics. Cambridge University Press 2012.

Taylor, Robert S. *Exit Left: Markets and Mobility in Republican Thought*. Oxford University Press 2017.

7

Freedom in the Workplace

Elizabeth Anderson

I first came across Elizabeth Anderson working through a reading list on equality during my MA. After pushing through a steady stream of lukewarm, narrow analysis, our discussion group collectively encountered her "What Is the Point of Equality?" as a blast of fresh air. From its first sentence—"If much recent academic work defending equality had been secretly penned by conservatives, could the results be any more embarrassing for egalitarians?"—to its last, the piece seemed to cut through the (sometimes stale) debates on the topic with total ethical clarity.

More recently I came back to Professor Anderson's work doing my podcast. I often complained on the show that political philosophy, while very focused on the power states have over us, almost completely ignores the power employers have over our lives.

Like most generalizations, this was more than a little unfair. Many works by political philosophers and theorists have taken on the topic. The most prominent (deservedly) is Anderson's *Private Government*. Covering history, philosophy, and a response to critics in enviably lucid prose, it's true essential reading.

This chapter is based on my first interview with Professor Anderson. We start with *Private Government*—Anderson argues that the workplace is a site government: where power is exercised over us, government exists. If we ask what type of government workplaces are, it is clear that the vast majority are dictatorships. I bring up the main counterarguments—surely, we can leave bad jobs and freely negotiate the terms of employment elsewhere—and

Elizabeth Anderson, *Freedom in the Workplace* In: *What is Freedom?*. Edited by: Toby Buckle, Oxford University Press. © Oxford University Press 2021. DOI: 10.1093/oso/9780197572214.003.0008

Anderson responds. This is followed by a discussion of why this topic has been comparatively neglected by political philosophy.

Elizabeth Anderson is the John Dewey Distinguished University Professor, John Rawls Collegiate Professor, and Arthur F. Thurnau Professor at the University of Michigan. She specializes in ethics, social and political philosophy, feminist theory, social epistemology, and the philosophy of economics and the social sciences. She has a strong interest in the interactions of social science with moral and political theory, how we learn to improve our value judgments, the epistemic functions of emotions and democratic deliberation, and issues of race, gender, and equality.

She is the author of *Value in Ethics and Economics*, *The Imperative of Integration*, and, most recently, *Private Government: How Employers Rule Our Lives (And Why We Don't Talk about It)*, as well as articles on value theory, the ethical limitations of markets, facts and values in social scientific research, feminist and social epistemology, racial integration and affirmative action, rational choice and social norms, democratic theory, egalitarianism, and the history of ethics (focusing on Kant, Mill, and Dewey).

What is the central thesis of *Private Government*?
The key idea is that we have to recognize the workplace as a site of government. You have bosses who are ruling over workers, issuing them orders and threatening to do bad things to them if they don't follow those orders. Maybe they'll get fired, or demoted, or just yelled at.

When you are subject to orders and have to obey on threat of sanction, you are subject to government. So that way of understanding things allows us to apply the tools of political philosophy to a site where it hasn't usually been applied. As you know, most political philosophers are obsessed with the state and ignore authority in other domains outside of it. I want to highlight the fact that you have millions of workers who are suffering under bosses, who are being very abusive, controlling and interfering with their autonomy, even off duty. It's a problem that's pervasive, especially in the American workplace.

You can ask: if the workplace is a site of government, what is the constitution of that government? Well, it's certainly not a democracy.

There's a handful of firms which have a democratic organization, but that's rare in America. The constitution of the government of the workplace is a dictatorship in which the bosses have virtually unaccountable power over the workers. The workers don't really have much recourse to hold their bosses to account. They don't have a voice within the government of the workplace. That's what I call private government; when the government is kept private *from* those who are ruled by it and it is treated by the rulers as just their own private matter.

Many people would say the workplace is nothing like the government because the state can imprison you, whereas you can just go find another job if you don't like it.

People could emigrate from Italy under Mussolini. We don't say that therefore it was a democracy. It's still a dictatorship.

Within the EU there's freedom of movement, people not only have the right to exit any country in the EU, but they actually have the right to enter other countries in the EU. But we don't think that government has ended on account of that. It's the same for the vast majority of workers; self-employment is not a credible option to make a living and so really the only options are hopping from one dictatorship to the next. The right of exit does not change the constitution of the government.

Also, especially in the States, the cost of exit can be really quite high because, for instance, our healthcare tends to be tied to our employment. So, you can say you're free to leave, but if you have a child who is reliant on your healthcare, that's a very precarious sort of freedom.

Quite right. Government does not only exist when there's a power to imprison or execute you. There are weaker forms of government, but even the weaker forms, such as we find in the workplace, can still impose terrible costs on workers. That's why they put up with mountains of abuse: because the costs of exit can be extremely high and they have no assurance that if they moved to a different firm things would be any better.

To illustrate: about 90% of servers in restaurants are subject to sexual harassment. It's such a pervasive problem that just moving from one restaurant to the next isn't really going to offer any assurance that one will be able to escape it.

What about the argument that employment is a freely negotiated contract between two parties that both agreed to?
I think the critical issue here is that the terms of employment are dictated by the employer. It's a rare case where one is represented by a collective bargaining unit, a union, or one has the skills that put one in a position to do any negotiating. In the vast majority of employment situations the employee just has to accept whatever is offered. The default employment contract was written by the state, and the state deals all the authority cards to the employer and none to the worker. That's underwritten by labor law and it creates this incredible asymmetry. Even the few legal rights that workers have are so dangerous for them to exercise that they frequently just hold their tongue. It is supposedly a guaranteed right of workers to complain about working conditions, even if they are not represented by a labor union. But it's so dangerous to speak out against the boss who could fire you, that most workers don't do that.

Which leads to a huge concentration of power that's absolutely unchallengeable. Say what you will about our politicians, at least in theory we can vote them out of office. There is nothing you can do to challenge the power of a manager. You can file an HR complaint or something, but . . .

It's dangerous! 70% of workers who complain about sexual harassment at work face retaliation. No wonder they're keeping silent! The vast majority of such cases never even come forth.

On top of that, in the United States, mandatory arbitration agreements are now forced on workers. That means that they have to take their complaint to an arbitrator who has a contract with the employer, not the employees. We have excellent data on how private sector arbitrators work. They return judgements in favor of the employer vastly more frequently than workers who get to sue their employer in court.

And, as you say, every worker doing an entry level job in America knows that making a complaint means putting a target on your back. Most midlevel people, or even senior people, don't want to speak up either, because they know their power in that institution is built on their relationships.

Oh, completely. The people in the middle also probably have aspirations to rise up in the organization, and being seen as a troublemaker and a boat-rocker, or a so called disgruntled employee, is not good for your career prospects.

Then finally there's the people at the very top. I'm not convinced, and there's a good deal in the history of political thought to back this up, that having that much unaccountable power is good for people.

Part of what's happened with the deregulated untrammeled capitalism that's emerged is the all-out assault on labor unions and the power of workers. This is going to corrupt the people at the top. It makes them ignorant of what's going on, because workers are afraid to complain. On top of that, when workers are disempowered, there's also a selection effect at the top. The narcissist, the megalomaniac now sees an open path to power. Whereas before, when executives had to operate under greater constraints and pushback, the type of people who would select those roles were actually more morally responsive people. Now we have more total predators up at the top.

Who, as tyrants tend to do, often surround themselves with sycophants.

I think there's a lot to be said for that. Certainly in many, many firms, you see that kind of culture emerging. But I also do want to stress that there's a wide variety of corporate cultures. It's not uniformly awful. There are some really well managed firms that aren't relentlessly abusive to their workers. That's one of the reasons why we don't see every last worker complaining about their situation, or even aware that they're living under a dictatorship, because, for a lot of workers, the work conditions are pretty good.

Of course, different workers within the firm experience different kinds of power exercised on them. Generally speaking, the higher up you are, the better things are for you and the less abusive the power is. It's the lower level workers (who are easily replaced), the entry level workers, "unskilled" workers, and so forth who tend to suffer most.

With respect to the executives who do act badly though, I think it can be both an ego thing and a single-minded focus on profits. I think an interesting example of this would be Tesla making their electric cars. Reviews indicate that at least their high-end model is a spectacular car and an unbelievably fun drive. So as a piece of technology, it's quite impressive, but Elon Musk himself is a bit of a megalomaniac. One of the public lessons of this is that there's no safety in his assembly plant because it's speed at all costs. He realizes that the company needs to expand its market and to hell with worker safety. There's tons of accidents. People are injured and he just doesn't care.

Then you also have some executives who are spreadsheet managers. They have no connection to the conditions on the ground. They're just trying to push numbers, I don't even think it's ego for them. They've got numbers they want to hit and they don't care how this happens. Look at Boeing, for instance. The Boeing managers are not publicity hogs, but they were just so driven by this need to deliver the 737 Max. Safety went out the window. Safety for passengers, we're not even talking just about the workers here. They had deadlines, they had production schedules, they just had to get things done so they could book their profits. It's all about moving the numbers. In fact, they were remarkably detached, shockingly detached from the passengers, from the engineers, from the actual assembly plant; they didn't care. They just said. "deliver the goods." If they were defective products, that didn't matter.

Do you think there's anything to the idea that a lot of the anger we're seeing in our politics comes from people feeling humiliated by both the material conditions of their employment, and by the powerlessness of many jobs?

The fact that neoliberalism took over even the center-left political parties, certainly made people think "nobody cares" about us. Right. The Democratic Party basically went over to neoliberalism under Clinton; that was its political strategy. It led to these free trade agreements which had a devastating effect on manufacturing employment in the United States. If you look at the counties that shifted in the 2016 election from having voted for Obama in 2008, to flipping to Trump in 2016, a lot of them are rural former manufacturing centers where people lost jobs. This was mostly due to China's accession to the World Trade Organization and the overpowering competitiveness of low-wage Chinese manufacturing, which led to the shutdown of US plants.

People argue about the impact of economics versus racism in Trump's victory, what's your view on that?

The racist elements are prominent. This is an old playbook that was created in the 19th century, in struggles over the abolition of slavery. You had John C. Calhoun, a famous proslavery senator and a very powerful politician in the United States government, defending slavery against the antislavery sentiments up North. Abraham Lincoln's antislavery argument was not just that slavery was wrong. It was of course an injustice to the slave. But it also undermined the interests of free White workers. His argument was that if slaves do manual labor, then anyone doing manual labor gets demeaned and stigmatized because they're doing slave work. Also, there was a material benefit that free workers had in ensuring that everyone is a free worker; they wouldn't have to compete against slave labor.

This was a particular concern out West, where there were still territories open for settlement. Lincoln argued that if you let slave owners go out to these territories, they'll create giant plantations with hundreds of slaves and displace opportunities for free workers to stake out a homestead on their own.

Calhoun, in response, wrote a very famous speech. He said that northerners don't understand how things work in the South among Whites. Whether they owned slaves or not, whether they're rich or poor, they all enjoy a status of equality in virtue of being White:

> Can as much, on the score of equality, be said of the North? With us the two great divisions of society are not the rich and poor, but White and Black; and all the former, the poor as well as the rich, belong to the upper class, and are respected and treated as equals, if honest and industrious; and hence have a position and pride of character of which neither poverty nor misfortune can deprive them.

What Calhoun was saying to poor Whites, who are economically exploited and trampled down by the economic system, is we're offering you a better bargain than northerners. Yes you're going to be poor. But at the end of the day you still get to trample all over Blacks. You have racial privilege. You'll get all these symbolic benefits we're offering you in virtue of being White. That's a kind of consolation prize for the fact that you are in poverty and desperate.

It's a persuasive argument to many Whites. We still have Whites today who are voting against their material interests because they have a deeper stake in whiteness and white privilege; in this symbolic state. They took that bargain. Meanwhile their pockets are getting picked by the plutocrats, but they're okay with that as long as they get a higher status from whiteness.

There's also a fear element. That's extremely important. If anything, I think fear is more dominant than sadism in today's politics. This idea that people of color are going to be a demographic majority and that Whites are going to be shut out of power. That's terrifying, I think, for many Trump voters.

Of course, it's a perverse fantasy, but it's been passed down for generations.

Would that also apply to the anti-immigration rhetoric we've seen?

It's very fear driven, and the fear is coming from places where people don't even have a lot of contact with immigrants. It's not surprising that the big cosmopolitan locations welcome immigrants, because that's where most of them are. City people develop a skill set from interacting with people who come from different places. Then they're okay with that.

You go out to more rural areas, where encountering immigrants is not all that common, people don't have that skill set. They're frankly afraid, they're really uncomfortable. To give you an example, I was talking with a former member of the philosophy department staff some months ago, who I know lives in a rural area and is a Trump voter.

She had recently switched jobs. She got a bigger job with more pay in the Department of Romance Languages. So they're people from France, Italy, Spain, and so forth that she's working with. I asked how the new job was working out for her. She did like the higher pay and the greater responsibility. But she said, "I always wonder, out in the hallway, people are speaking French and Spanish and Italian, are they talking about me? What are they saying about me?'

That just really gave me an insight into the mind of people who are troubled by immigration. They think why would anyone speak another language? Because they want to say something bad about you. Now actually people are talking these languages because they're here to study them, many of them are native speakers, and others are students practicing them.

She's coming from a different world in which that fear and suspicion is commonplace because she isn't used to interacting with different people. I think actually she might even get over it and, over time, get used to having interactions with the people in her new department. At least I hope she will learn. The evidence does show that people do learn, if they're in the right setting. That's one of the genius features of the contemporary metropolis is that people acquire those skill sets. And then they're cool with immigrants because there are opportunities for positive engagement on both sides.

I think the American right, in creating a mythology that elevates the virtues of rural life, can often ignore or stigmatize the great things about cities. Cities can be incredible engines of integration and cultural exchange.

So, I think it's a complicated issue. In certain ways they are engines of integration for immigrants. But the scale of anti-Black racism can never be exaggerated in America, and you do see that in cities. It interacts strongly with class inequality. If you look at the major metropolitan areas, places like New York City, Chicago, you have super rich people, and then you have very poor people, and that correlates closely with race.

The rich people are sending their kids to private schools, which are virtually all White, and the public schools have been left to Black, Latino, and immigrant children. And of course they're underfunded because the people with the money aren't sending their kids there, so what do they care?

But the answer to that is more integration. Right?

I think that that's what you have to do. That's why I favor affirmative action at the university level, although, to tell you the truth, it's coming way too late. We really need integration in grades K through 12, but that's where the parents tend to be most panicky. The fears are not grounded in reality; they're grounded in centuries of racist propaganda.

This is also an area that allows us to combine concerns about racial inequality with the concerns about workers. One of the most important sites of racial integration is in labor unions. There's also a lot of racism there. But many unions learned their lesson: when they tried to be all White, corporations would hire Black strikebreakers. There's no path forward for unions without racial integration. The first large-scale labor movement in the United States, which started shortly after the end of the Civil War, was the Knights of Labor, which opposed anti-Black racism. It racially integrated Black and White workers, although it excluded Chinese workers. Antiracism is a lesson that the American labor movement has had to learn over and over again.

The destruction of labor unions has been a disaster because they have been one of the most important sites for multiracial coalition and movement building outside the context of a formal political party. Political parties can't do all the political acts. They have a function, but especially if they're on the left, they need social movements independent of the party to push them to do the right thing.

It seems to me that contemporary political philosophy has focused very much on the distribution of material goods, and much less on other political currencies such as exclusion, honor, degradation, humiliation, and so on.

I agree with that. Although I do think that matters are changing; for the longest time basically everything was about distribution of income, wealth, and opportunities. There was very, very little reflection on power outside of the state. You just had a kind of bland, liberal consensus that wasn't really focusing on what the problems were in peoples' experiences. I do think that that's changing, we're seeing a revival of republican theory and people started to apply that to the workplace outside the context of the state.

You write in *Private Government*:

No doubt, many of us, especially most who are reading these lectures, do not find the situation so bad. My readers are most likely tenured or tenure track professors who almost uniquely among organized workers in the United States enjoy due process rights and a level of autonomy at work that is unmatched almost anywhere else among employees.

That seems to me a really plausible explanation as to why political philosophers focus quite a lot on income inequality, but comparatively less on inequality of power: academics aren't the richest people in society, but they are protected from abusive power to a much greater degree than most other workers.

They should be talking to their colleagues who are adjuncts. Adjunct instructors are some of the most exploited, downtrodden people around. People have no idea how awful their conditions are. Many adjuncts are paid just a couple thousand dollars per course, well below minimum wage. It's shocking that that's even permitted, and they don't have much autonomy either, given that they're on contingent contracts.

They don't feel free to speak up against anything that's done to them in the workplace or against any kind of arbitrary treatment. If only the tenured ones had more communication with the adjuncts, maybe they would learn a lot about academic work. That is the actual conditions of work for the people who are teaching most college students.

I also want to point out that the place where I think contemporary political philosophy really started to think critically about power is among feminist philosophers and philosophers of color. Domination and power have been on the agenda for a long time in those fields, for example in the feminist slogan that "the personal is political." Feminist philosophy has really been an inspiration for a lot of political theory, thinking about the conditions of, not just women, but people of color and any kind of marginalized or oppressed group. There's a lot of productive work on that, for instance Charles Mills writing about the contract and domination.

So issues of power and domination outside of the context of the state have definitely been explored, but not really by the sort of generic mainstream political philosophy where we're just liberals duking it out with libertarians. Certainly in feminist theory and critical race theory you see a lot more attention to issues of domination.

That's where I was going with that: If an academic's environment might influence their research, isn't that an argument for diversity?

Absolutely. I mean, it's often hard to see your power and privilege if you occupy it. It just seems normal that this is how people should be treated. So yes, there's a clear intellectual case for diversifying academia with people coming from different social situations. They'll ask different questions, notice different problems, try out different methods. That's what happens when you have first-person access to different aspects of social reality, if you explore different things, then that gives us a fuller picture of what's really going on.

Would that be an argument for a diversity in who's producing philosophy which, in addition to a diversity of demographic

identities, also aims to consider views from people with diverse work and career backgrounds?

It's really interesting. I'm all in favor of expanding the canon. Especially in political philosophy there's a lot of pamphlets, literature, etc., that articulate alternative perspectives that haven't been canonized. It's really worth engaging with that stuff. The Levellers in the 17th century were not canonized, but boy they're damn good political philosophers. Have you ever read the Putney debates?

No

Everybody should read the Putney debates. These are great because what they show is how sharp and smart ordinary people can be if they're confronted with a matter of extreme urgency. These are not academics, but it's political philosophy carried out at a level of sophistication that's as good as anything you're going to read in the canon, and with very real stakes.

In the mid 17th century in the English Civil War, the King had been captured by the army, and the representatives of the New Model Army met in Putney with Cromwell to discuss what they should do with the King, and what the new constitution should look like.

The Levellers presented a republican constitution. They wanted to abolish the House of Lords and its privileges. They wanted a universal franchise. It's a radical democratic agenda. Cromwell was more conservative, and so they had these amazing arguments about things like the franchise. How broad should it be? Would it be a universal male franchise? (They're not talking about franchising women!)

So, the Putney debates are three days of debate, taken down verbatim (by an excellent scribe). In them you see how ordinary people can engage in political philosophy at a high level of sophistication. Days two and three are where they really get to the guts of the constitution. We know the debates continued for a couple of extra days, but for some reason we don't have a transcription after day three.

What we do have though is powerful, noncanonical stuff that really ought to be canonized; just ordinary soldiers arguing with the powers that be.

When I teach, I like to mix up canonical and noncanonical authors and have them argue with each other. For example, a really great author, a very, very shrewd political psychologist is Frederick Douglass. A fugitive slave, then a free person arguing against slavery. This guy's amazingly smart, incredibly sharp, and a fantastic writer. He blows away so many other writers of his era. He's a political actor of enormous import, before, during, and after the Civil War. So, his writing certainly should be in the canon of political philosophy.

People argue that historically, most political theory works were written by rich White guys, so that's what we teach.

People say that in ignorance. There's a lot of archival work going on now. There's flourishing historical research on early modern philosophy which is digging up a lot of women philosophers in the early modern period. These are really interesting people, and once you bring them back in, it suddenly shifts your view of what was going on in the 17th and 18th centuries. Women were engaged in not just political philosophy, but also in metaphysics and epistemology. So, I think a lot of pronouncements that it was all just guys, and that's just how it was, are really based on ignorance.

Further Reading

Anderson, Elizabeth. *Private Government: How Employers Rule Our Lives (and Why We Don't Talk about It)*. Princeton University Press 2007.
Anderson, Elizabeth. *The Imperative of Integration*. Princeton University Press 2013.

PART III
ACTIVISM

8

LGBT Liberation

Peter Tatchell

Peter Tatchell is something of a personal moral compass for me. As a lifelong activist he has consistently identified, exposed, and worked to change the injustices of the eras through which he's lived. His work today remains both courageous and possessing of a focused ethical clarity that is virtually unmatched.

Peter is widely recognized as one of the United Kingdom's most prominent and influential human rights campaigners. Among his many involvements, he was a leading activist in the Gay Liberation Front 1971–1974 and in the queer human rights group OutRage! 1990–2011.

From confronting Mike Tyson, to attempting a "citizen's arrest" of Robert Mugabe, to jumping in front of Tony Blair's motorcade, to being badly assaulted as part of Moscow Gay Pride, Peter has put his personal safety at risk, time and time again, to call attention to human rights abuses.

Through the Peter Tatchell Foundation, he currently campaigns for human rights in Britain and internationally.

Peter's key political inspirations are Mahatma Gandhi, Sylvia Pankhurst, Martin Luther King, and, to some extent, Malcolm X and Rosa Luxemburg. He has adapted many of their methods to his contemporary nonviolent struggle for human rights—and invented a few of his own.

He is the author of over three thousand published articles and six books, including *The Battle for Bermondsey*, *Democratic Defence—A Non-Nuclear Alternative*, and *We Don't Want to March*

Peter Tatchell, *LGBT Liberation* In: *What is Freedom?*. Edited by: Toby Buckle, Oxford University Press.
© Oxford University Press 2021. DOI: 10.1093/oso/9780197572214.003.0009

Straight—Masculinity, Queers and the Military. His ground-breaking book, *AIDS: A Guide to Survival*, published in 1986, was the world's first self-help guide for people with HIV. It challenged the then consensus that AIDS equals death.

Awards won by Peter Tatchell include Observer Ethical Awards Campaigner of the Year 2009, Blue Plaque 2010, Irwin Prize—Secularist of the Year 2012, Gandhi International Peace Award 2016, and Albert Medal 2016.

When he was on the podcast, we discussed liberation versus equality as overarching goals for LGBTQ movements.

You've said that when you started campaigning you never talked about equality, you talked about liberation. Could you explain the distinction?

When I first began my human rights and LGBT+ campaigning in the late 1960s, it was from a place of very grave oppression. In many countries, including many western countries, homosexuality was still totally criminalized. You could be jailed, forced to undergo compulsory psychiatric treatment, fired from your job, and evicted from your home. When I got involved in the early gay liberation movement, our agenda was very much about questioning and critiquing society. Although we opposed anti-LGBT+ discrimination, the word "equality" never passed our lips. Our concern was to transform society, to not only liberate LGBT+ people, but also straight people as well.

We saw this transformative agenda as going way beyond the narrow confines of equal rights. Basically, if you only seek equality, you're asking for equal rights within the existing status quo. Our argument was that the status quo is flawed. We did not want equality within a fundamentally unjust system. Our goal was to transform the system to liberate everyone and, to achieve this, build alliances between different social movements, so that we could all work together to change society for everyone's benefit.

That's so different from when I started doing social justice work (about ten years ago), for us, "equality" was the watchword. Marriage equality for instance. How would your argument cover that?

I was one of the people who began the campaign for marriage equality in the UK way back in the late eighties and early nineties—but not because I was a fan of wedlock. In fact, I share the feminist critique of marriage as a fundamentally patriarchal institution with a rather tragic history of oppressing both women and LGBT+ people. However, I obviously opposed discrimination in marriage law because it was homophobic. So, even though I personally would not want to get married and even though I'm a critic of marriage, I opposed the ban on same-sex couples having that choice, because our exclusion was inspired by homophobia. Simultaneously, I also argued for an alternative both to marriage and civil unions. Civil unions are, in essence, marriage by another name, replicating the same basic template. What I was suggesting is that, yes, let's get rid of homophobic discrimination in marriage law, but let's also aspire to something much better.

If we were starting from scratch, I doubt that people today would go for the marriage model. I think they'd try and find something that was more modern, egalitarian, and flexible—and more attuned to modern people's loves and lifestyles. For example, under my proposed alternative to marriage and civil unions—what I've called a civil commitment pact—I've suggested that anyone should be able to nominate any "significant other" person in their life as next of kin and inheritance beneficiary. At the moment, there's discrimination against single people: only those in marriages and civil unions, formalized by law, are automatically next of kin to their partner. Moreover, when one partner in a marriage or civil union dies, the surviving partner has huge tax exemptions in terms of the inheritance of property and wealth. Single people don't have those advantages. My scheme would remedy that.

Moreover, in the case of couples in a romantic love relationship, the partners should be able to jointly pick and mix from a menu of rights and responsibilities. The problem with marriage and civil unions is that it's one size fits all. They're written in stone, there's no negotiation and no option to amend the contract. You just sign the pregiven terms and conditions. Under my system, the partners would be able to sit down and negotiate each individual right and responsibility. This is important because we are not all the same. Some couples may want to have joint guardianship of children, others may not. While some live together, others live separately. Some may want to share their finances, others might prefer to maintain financial independence. There's a whole host of different variations in the way couples live and relate. So under my system, couples would have access to a menu of rights and responsibilities from which they can pick and choose, in order to create a tailor-made partnership agreement suited to their particular needs. I think that's better and fairer.

Also, it might actually help concentrate the mind. If partners had to sit down and negotiate each aspect of their mutual rights and responsibilities, I think they would be better apprised about what they were getting into. So it might lead to wiser and more considered decisions.

I'm not saying that this idea of mine is the be all and end all. I'm just saying it's perhaps the beginning of a debate about possible alternatives to marriage and civil unions. We should not assume that what's been handed down to us by history is what should stay, what should exist forever as the one and only way to recognize love and commitment.

I can imagine a conservative saying; people have been getting married this way for all of human history and now you want to throw it out of the window? Who knows what's coming down the line if you do that.

I'm not proposing to abolish marriage. Some people might, but I'm not. I'm saying this alternative would be an addition to what currently exists, to give people a third option. We should try to create a system that will work for, and have the confidence of, people who are not enamored of marriage and civil unions. We have to think beyond marriage and marriage-lite civil unions. These are based on history and tradition, not on what actually accords with many people's needs today. For those who are not captivated by the traditional system of relationship recognition, give them an alternative.

Do you think there is any importance in maintaining traditions, even if they have problematic aspects? I also agree with the feminist critique of marriage, yet found the gathering of friends and family, the exchanging of vows, and so on, in my own marriage ceremony to be deeply meaningful.

I think a lot of people like the ritual of marriage and civil unions. My alternative model of relationship recognition or rights could have ceremony and ritual if that is what people want. You could still have a wedding-like get together with friends, family, and loved ones. I'm just trying to reframe the legal structure rights and responsibilities in a different, modern way. As I mentioned, today there is a huge variety of relationships: some partners live together, others live apart; some share their finances, others maintain financial independence; some have kids, others don't. My new framework is trying to accommodate all those different variations and, at the same time, give people a genuine choice about what rights and what responsibilities they want to enter into and commit to.

For those who want marriage and civil unions, I wish them well and I'll defend their right to that. I champion the right of same-sex and opposite-sex couples to get married if they wish, despite my own personal reservations about the institution. So it's not about me trying to impose my will on others. It's just coming up with an alternative model and opening it up for people who want to take advantage of it.

Do you think it would be popular? I could well have seen myself going down that route. If it had been an option on the table.

When I've spoken and written about the idea, there's been a sizable minority of people who've said, "Yeah, that sounds more like me" and "That sounds like the kind of relationship framework I would like." Now there are others who say, "no, no, no, marriage is the gold standard." That's fine for them as well. The point is to give people a choice and not force them to accept the traditional idea about what constitutes a legally valid relationship.

Libertarians often say the government should have no role in marriage at all: People should just form whatever contracts they want with each other.

Contracts work up to a point; but no amount of contractual agreement and obligation between two people can get around the inheritance tax and social security laws. Also, immigrating to a different country, care of children, and things like that, cannot be resolved by couple contracts. A contract does not necessarily deal with some of the problems that can result from an ugly breakup. So we should have a system of law governing relationships for those who want it, precisely in order to cater for those unforeseen circumstances; the circumstances where a more vulnerable party could be left high and dry by a more dominant, powerful, or wealthy partner.

Staying with the theme of liberation versus equality, one area where you've argued you wouldn't want equality is sex education.

If the goal of LGBT+ activism is merely that same-sex relations are covered just as well in sex education as heterosexual relations, then that would still be a pretty sad outcome, right?

Absolutely.

The quality of sex education in most schools is woefully inadequate. Young people say this themselves. It's not me making this point; it's young people saying they're not getting enough information. Sex education is mostly biological. It's often about reproduction, not about emotions. It's rarely about things like how to deal with problems in a relationship. The emotional side is mostly ignored. It's certainly not about how to have good quality sex and how to satisfy your partner—the things that are the building blocks of a happy, fulfilled relationship. There is also not enough teaching about consent and abuse issues to protect young people from peer pressure and sexual exploitation.

We all know that for most people, the person they love and have a relationship with is one of the most important things in their lives. Yet we also know (and surveys show) that many couples are emotionally and sexually unfulfilled. I'm not saying teaching about these issues in schools is a panacea. However, we certainly do know that in countries, and in some schools in Britain, where this has been trialed, it leads to more responsible sexual behavior, including fewer teenage pregnancies and abortions; lower rates of sexually transmitted infections, including HIV; and a higher level of sexual and emotional satisfaction in relationships. These outcomes suggest that early, high-quality sex and relationship education is good for the individual, the couple, and the wider society; because happy fulfilled couples and relationships make for a better society.

I just think it's really weird that anybody would want equality within what currently exists in sex and relationship education, given how inadequate it mostly is.

I certainly agree that sex education is also inadequate for straight people. From what I've heard from female friends particularly, or read in writings on this by women, it appears many young men lack quite basic knowledge.

We know in Britain, from many surveys over the years, that there are fairly modest levels of sexual and emotional satisfaction in both casual and married relationships. And you're right, that is often because their partners don't know, don't listen, and don't understand. They've never been told. With teenage boys, for example: "What is the clitoris? Where is the clitoris?" I remember I did some school lessons and the number of boys who knew what the clitoris was and where it was, was very, very low—about 10% of a class of about a hundred. With this level of ignorance, no wonder women often feel unfulfilled by sex.

This is partly about challenging ignorance and imparting knowledge. It's also about challenging macho attitudes among some young men. This macho bravado toward sex, the sex of conquest and bragging, often indicates a lack of awareness, sensitivity and mutuality in a relationship. That needs to change. I'm not saying schools are the panacea, but schools are a good place to start.

Where this kind of education has been tried, it does seem to improve things. I think we need to create an education system that prepares young people, as a school system is supposed to, for adult life. One aspect of adult life, and a very important one, is sex and relationships. The idea that people should be literate in English and maths, but not in sex and relationships, strikes me as absurd.

You've advocated for teaching sexual techniques, including for types of sex other than intercourse. I can imagine some parents being horrified by the idea of, say, teaching their children how to perform oral sex.

When I've spoken about this publicly, it has initially provoked outrage, but I've turned to parents and said:

"As a parent, you want the best for your child. You know that sexual intercourse carries higher risks than oral sex and mutual masturbation. Surely you would prefer your child to engage in low risk behavior rather than high risk behavior? Surely you want your child to know and understand about safer sex?"

Sometimes, not every time, but sometimes, they calm down and then there's a conversation. When they hear the evidence and aim of this education, they're less shocked and horrified. They're more open to consideration.

We know that among young people who have oral sex and mutual masturbation, the levels of unwanted pregnancies and sexually transmitted infections is much lower. I'm sure that has to be a good thing.

I always say to everyone, I don't encourage young people to have sex. I think it's best if they wait. For me, speaking personally, sex is usually better and more fulfilling within the context of a relationship, but that's not the way lots of young people think and behave. So how can we focus on harm reduction? How can we reduce the chances of them doing themselves and their partners harm? How can we in particular reduce the levels of teen pregnancies, abortions, and sexual infections?

If promoting alternatives to intercourse is one way to do it, then surely it is in the interest of young people's welfare that we do so.

I agree, I just think there's this fear many people have of anything that puts children and sex in the same sentence.

Yeah, and in this day and age, when we are rightly concerned about the shocking levels of child sexual abuse, to keep young people in ignorance about sex colludes with their abusers. I find it so shocking that in Britain there are very few examples of schools who actually talk to their pupils about sexual abuse issues. Quite a few will say, well, phone Childline, but that's not good enough. Phoning Childline (which is a helpline for young people who have a problem), is fine, but it's clearly not adequate. The problem is that sexual abusers utilize guilt and shame about sex in order to silence victims and continue their abuse. Young people who aren't confident talking about sex, who feel guilt and shame, will be less likely to say no to abusers, and less likely to speak out to their teachers or parents. They will keep it hidden, which is exactly what the abuser wants. So challenging sexual guilt and shame is part of the armory of protecting and empowering people against sexual abuse.

So marriage law and sex education are two concreate examples of where "liberation" would seem to capture your goals better than "equality." What's changed in LGBT movements that we've gone from talking about the former to the latter?

I think the LGBT+ liberation movements that grew up in Britain, the United States, and other western countries in the late sixties and early seventies were very much movements of an era of idealism and radicalism, when authority and tradition were being challenged. You had the rise of the Black liberation movement, the women's liberation movement, and the LGBT+ liberation movement as well. All these movements were taking on people in power and authority, challenging laws and traditions, as well as taking on social institutions that marginalized respectively, Black people, women, and LGBT+ people.

I think what happened is that some people in the movement found that the quest for a liberation agenda, for social transformation, was too big an ask. They thought "let's lower our horizons to the more easily achievable goal of equality." Equal rights has got a better ring to it, it's got more popular appeal, it's more possible than the huge task of transforming society. So we had this lowering of expectations, hopes and aspirations to the more limited goal of equal rights within society as it exists.

And of course this was fueled by the fact that more and more LGBT+ people began to professionally get into positions of power, where they had to play the system and were expected to work within it. This meant that lots of people who previously were in the LGBT+ liberation movement, thought "liberation" is a tough ask. They reasoned that the goal of fundamentally transforming society was not making much progress, so let's go for equal employment rights, an end to criminalization and so on. I can understand that, to a point. I don't think the two are necessarily mutually exclusive. You can fight for reform and also have the longer term goal of systemic structural social change.

I think the big danger of the equality agenda is that it can ultimately lead to the collapse of the movement. If you take the struggle of African Americans as an example; it was all premised on equal rights: equal voting rights and an end to segregation in the deep South. Once those narrow equal treatment goals were won, the movement collapsed. Yet here we are, more than half a century later, and you could reasonably argue that in some parts of the US informal segregation based on race is almost as bad as it was in the 1950s and '60s. There's a whole section of the African American population who are still locked out of economic prosperity and success.

So, racism hasn't gone away and racial injustice is still with us, even though the laws have changed and so have many institutions—but not far enough. Witness the wave of police murders of unarmed Black people. African Americans still get a raw deal. They're still not truly and genuinely respected and accepted. There are not the kind of equal outcomes that Martin Luther King aspired to. That's why he, particularly toward the end of his life, also focused on economic justice. He said that was a key element of the struggle for Black rights, that mere equality within the law was not adequate.

I believe we're seeing a very similar scenario with the LGBT+ movement. In Britain, up until 1999, we had, by volume, the largest number of antigay laws of any country in the world, some dating back centuries. Today we have some of the best laws. That's a fantastic, phenomenal, extraordinary achievement. It's the fastest, most successful law reform campaign in British, and possibly world, history. I can't think of another example where so many laws affecting a discriminated minority have been repealed in such a short space of time. But the consequence is that in the wake of these victories the LGBT+ movement and campaign organizations have diminished. There are still some organizations, but nowhere near the number and the scale of three decades ago. Yet there are many issues still remaining that need to be addressed, and there is not the movement and community infrastructure to adequately remedy them.

Do you think there's a difference in how effective the terms are in motivating people to take action? You said that equality has a broader appeal, but I can also see liberation as being more inspiring, albeit perhaps for a smaller number of people.

Different people will be inspired in different ways and I don't want to dismiss or disparage those who stick with the equality mantra. All I'm saying is, I don't think it's adequate and I don't think it has fulfilled our objectives. There are lots of issues within our own community that have got nothing to do with equality, or very little to do with it. It includes things like how we treat each other within our community, such as the marginalization of Black, disabled, bisexual, trans, and nonbinary LGBTs, and the problematic youth- and sex-obsessed culture that we ourselves have created.

Likewise, look at the high rates of mental ill-health within our community. A lot of it is the result of homophobia, biphobia, and transphobia, but our response is actually quite weak. There are few organizations in the LGBT+ community that address mental health issues affecting LGBT+ people, and yet it's a major issue. That's partly because we've put all our eggs in the basket of equality and law reform, rather than looking at LGBT lives in the round. The fact is that many of the issues and problems we face cannot simply be reduced to matters of equal rights and legal equality.

The value of freedom is often invoked by people on the other side of arguments over homophobia. For instance, claiming free speech or free expression protections for bigoted views and actions. How do you evaluate those claims?

I think that all bigoted ideas, whether they pertain to race, sex, disability, sexual orientation or gender identity, should be challenged and never be given a free pass. But where do we draw the line? Free speech is a very precious human right. I would say that it can only be legitimately limited in three scenarios:

First, where someone is making false, damaging allegations. So if, as a way of scoring a point, you're falsely claiming that a person is a pedophile or a tax fraudster, that is not free speech. That's an abuse of free speech, and no one should be allowed to do that.

Second, if someone is engaging in persistent harassment and threats. That's also an abuse of free speech.

Third, where people incite violence against other human beings. Some people will say that's free speech. I would say it's another abuse of free speech, which actually closes down speech because people who have violence incited against them will be cowed into silence. They won't feel able to exercise their freedom of speech and won't participate in the public debate because they will fear violent consequences.

For example, I was involved in the OutRage! "stop murder music" campaign against eight Jamaican reggae and dance hall singers who were advocating killing fellow Black people who were LGBT+. Critics accused me of censoring them and closing down their right to free speech. Well, first of all, incitement to violence is a serious criminal offense (and quite rightly so). It's not free speech, it's a crime. Secondly, those murder music lyrics, and those who advocated them, intimidated Black LGBT+ people from putting their head above the parapet and speaking out because they were afraid that they would be killed.

So I do believe that free speech can be sometimes legitimately limited in order to preserve genuine free speech for everyone.

What about "freedom" to refuse service, or to opt out of participating in something you disagree with? For example, the cases of bakers refusing to bake cakes for gay weddings.

I don't think anyone has a right to discriminate against a person by refusing to provide a service because of their race, gender, sexuality or whatever. That's clearly discrimination. In a free and democratic society we can't have people unilaterally deciding they are not going to serve this or that person because they're Jewish or Muslim or because they are Black or gay. That's unacceptable.

What is legitimate is that no one should be compelled to promote political messages they disagree with. For example, I opposed the prosecution of the Ashers Bakery in Northern Ireland. They did not refuse to serve Gareth Lee because he was a gay man; they refused to put on his cake the message "support gay marriage."

I'm really sad they took that stand. They are homophobes for opposing marriage equality. But I don't think they should be legally required to decorate a cake with a message to which they had a conscientious objection. It was a misguided conscientious objection, but a conscientious objection nonetheless. In the same sense, I don't think a gay baker should be forced by law to make a cake with a message opposing same-sex marriage. Discrimination against people is always wrong, but discrimination against an idea, either for or against equal marriage, is fair game in a liberal society. As the German communist Rosa Luxemburg argued: "Freedom must always mean freedom for those who think differently."

Further Reading

Lucas, Ian. *Outrage!: An Oral History*. Continuum (formerly Cassell Academic) 1998.

Power, Lisa. *No Bath but Plenty of Bubbles: Stories from the London Gay Liberation Front, 1970–73*. Continuum, International Publishing Group (formerly Cassell Academic) 1995.

For more information on Peter's work you can visit his foundation's website: petertatchellfoundation.org.

9

Windrush, Racism, and Freedom

Omar Khan

Omar Khan was Director of the Runnymede Trust, the UK's leading race equality thinktank for six years, until June 2020, and before that Head of Policy at Runnymede. In this capacity he was involved in helping bring the Windrush injustice to light and was a member of the advisory group of the Windrush Lessons Learned Review, chaired by Wendy Williams. He has written and spoken widely on race and racism in policy, academic, and media debates in Britain and internationally.

This interview was recorded specifically for this volume. Our aim was to combine an analysis of Windrush with a consideration of how progressive campaigners link their goals to political ideals such as justice, equality, and freedom. We start with an overview of Windrush; the history that led to that point, and how it was allowed to happen. Khan argues that what the episode shows, clearly, is that discrimination is not simply a matter of a few bad actors, but a systemic problem rooted in our history. Such discrimination is not merely unfair, or unjust, it is also a threat to our freedom: it constrains the choices people are able to make, how they are able to live their lives. The chapter ends with a consideration of how we might address racism, and what a truly free society would look like.

Who was the Windrush generation?
The Windrush generation is named after a ship, the *Empire Windrush*, which arrived in Tilbury Docks in June 1948. It's become a symbol of a wider phenomenon, which is the migration of

Omar Khan, *Windrush, Racism, and Freedom* In: *What is Freedom?*. Edited by: Toby Buckle, Oxford University Press. © Oxford University Press 2021. DOI: 10.1093/oso/9780197572214.003.0010 people from the Caribbean, but also from other parts of what was then still the British Empire to come and live and work in Britain after the Second World War.

There were, of course, Black people and other minorities living on these islands for hundreds of years, going back to the Roman times. But in the story of migration and British identity and how we became the nation that we are, the arrival of that ship in 1948 was a turning point in the numbers of people who arrived here.

Then what was the Windrush scandal that people talk about?
I would prefer to call it "the injustice" rather than scandal, because it wasn't, in my view, accidental or unexpected. In that sense, I think people were treated wrongly and badly in a predictable way.

The scandal emerged in terms of public consciousness in 2018. I think campaigners, activists, and obviously those affected, were aware that there were individuals who were being badly affected by the government's hostile environment policy, which had been implemented since around 2014 passed by the Cameron government when Theresa May was Home Secretary.

There were cases that were coming through where people who were living in Britain, sometimes British citizens for decades, were getting deported, detained, denied access to health treatments, denied access to employment, denied access to education, because they were unable to fulfill the new identity requirements to prove that they had lived in Britain in the ways that Home Office was now demanding. There were cases of people who had lived here, perfectly legally, since the 1960s or earlier, being threatened with deportation or denied access to cancer treatment.

In 2018 what happened was by collecting these, not as one-off cases, but as affecting a cohort of people, and applying the Windrush name, successfully and usefully as well as accurately. People saw that this wasn't a question of a few poor case decisions by the Home Office, but rather a structural problem with this policy.

What led to people being treated in this way?
The immediate or proximate cause was the hostile environment; a policy passed by the government in 2014 and 2016, purportedly about illegal immigration. In fact, the requirements of proving your identity, of being denied access to public services were extended to everyone. Of course, some people were less able to prove their identity than others.

To understand why it affected that Windrush cohort, we do have to go back to more historic causes than 2014 and 2016, which is the immigration and nationality law as it developed in Britain as we unraveled the empire.

The first Immigration Aliens Acts of 1905 was really targeting Jewish, eastern Europeans. The 1948 Immigration and Nationality Act was really the first one that outlined British nationality in that way. If you look at the dates, you can see the connection between the winding up of the empire and the passage of these bills.

India and Pakistan would become independent in 1947. There was a need in 1948 to specify that people from those places were no longer British and no longer had the rights to come. Then Jamaica became independent in 1962, along with Barbados and some of the other islands. So you have the 1962 Act and that's the first act that really puts serious controls on what we now call Commonwealth Immigration.

The 1968 Immigration Act introduced, and the 1971 Act extended, the concept of partiality to British Nationality Law, which is the requirement to show that your grandparent was born on this Island, not merely that your grandparent had a British passport. That is a key cause of the Windrush injustice, because the inequalities of rights that were wound up in empire had to be repatriated to Britain. We couldn't just allow everyone from the empire to land on these shores.

That is why this Windrush generation ran into trouble because they couldn't prove the new requirements of being British. It was always intended in the '71 Act that those who had come before '71 would be grandfathered in and would be allowed the basis of

British citizenship that existed before then. But all the changes that happened after '81 and particularly after the 2000s meant that those provisions that were supposed to protect this cohort from the new citizenship and immigration laws weren't effectively applied to them.

In addition, this group was relatively disadvantaged. Because of the racism and discrimination they experienced in the labor market, they weren't able to build up savings. Consequently, they hadn't been traveling back and forth to the Caribbean. They didn't need a passport.

The final thing is, if you went to secondary school in Jamaica, you studied the British curriculum, you studied and you studied English history. I remember speaking to one Windrush survivor who went to school in the late fifties in Jamaica. She told me that their exams were actually sent to England for marking.

They really did think they were British, not just legally, but emotionally and in terms of the culture that they grew up in. So I think to be told by people who are thirty years younger than them that they're not actually English (because they don't have the identity requirements that we decided that they need), I think was deeply insulting as well as morally and legally wrong.

When progressives talk about things we want to change, like everyone we reach for political concepts. For example you labeled these differential outcomes as unjust.
That tends to be where we go with discrimination or structural discrimination; we link it to justice. Is there a link to freedom? Can we say that living in a society which has structural discrimination makes you less free? If you can, what's the argument that gets you there?
Absolutely. Martin Luther King ends his famous "I Have a Dream" speech with "Let freedom ring." I think the civil rights movement very much focused on liberty. That discrimination constrains the ability of individuals to make the choices that they

otherwise would make. If we lived in society with less discrimination, people would be pursuing different things in their lives. Those things—where they live, how they work, their priorities in life— would be based on what they really want to do. So there would be more liberty.

We don't connect that argument well enough today. There has been a shift postwar, and especially on the left, to focus on equality and justice more.

I don't think the argument from liberty has ever disappeared. I think there's been a political alignment which means a lot of people on the left associate liberty with a narrow free market, libertarian conception of liberty. This I think, presents liberty incorrectly.

I would argue that racial discrimination is a greater source of unfreedom than taxation. The fact that many libertarians have spilled more ink over comparing taxation to slavery than discussing actual slavery and its real-world consequences is, in my view, a sign that they've got a blind spot for the historic and ongoing effects of enslavement.

What are the lessons of Windrush about discrimination, and by extension freedom, in the UK?
Windrush reveals racial discrimination as a systemic issue in Britain. It has deep roots in our history, our political and democratic institutions, and also in our culture. Our understanding of what race is, is not incidental either. We hold the same stereotypes and views that we held about Black people 200 years ago.

I think what Windrush reveals is the institutional nature of racial discrimination in Britain, the origin of those structures, and the beliefs that helped to justify those structures in terms of the inferiority of some groups because of their background.

But I think it also exposed some things that were more hidden, the institutional way that then affected people's rights and freedoms and liberties. The bit that is sometimes missed, is that the empire wasn't any state. It was a state that had different rights and privileges, depending on which bit you lived in. This was based on racialized groupings.

When the empire was unwound, those inequalities of rights and privileges were repatriated back to this Island. The successor to the state of empire became Britain. Which continues to be sustained by institutional practices, as well as by the same beliefs.

Thinking about that as an issue of liberty, those groups are unable to exercise the individual choices of what they want in their lives, where their children go to school, where they can choose to live. So it's not just about an individualist account of choice. It's also about rights and entitlements.

The individual account of liberty is sometimes perceived as just about economic, rationalist, choosers, but it's actually also about giving rights to those individuals that are most likely to need it, who are otherwise trampled by the state.

The counterargument from people opposed to "social justice" is they'll say, "By making discrimination structural, as opposed to individual, you've just created this huge, all encompassing, utterly unfalsifiable thing."

They would say sometimes differences in populations are entirely benign and we don't need to read prejudice into everything. The example that's always given is more White kids want to play baseball, more Black kids want to play basketball. You see differential outcomes. But in the absence of malign intent is that necessarily bad?

I think the shoe's on the other foot, I think they have to demonstrate why such disparities are not grounded in injustice, especially when we have such strong evidence. Anti-Black racism is not some minor obscure element in British or North American history. It has very deep roots.

Even with baseball and basketball, I'd be very happy to give an account of the different structural ways in which basketball was open to African Americans when baseball wasn't. For example, the infrastructure required: basketball is typically associated with playgrounds in cities whereas baseball fields were established in more suburban areas. Because there are big demographic differences between these different areas, Black and White Americans will have unequal access to sport infrastructure. Those demographic differences are the result of residential segregation patterns that are hardly free from discrimination.

The implications are quite extensive. I would agree with that point. I would just disagree that that's a problem. I am perfectly content to say that not all inequalities are derived from structural discrimination, and I'm perfectly content to say that we only want to attend to those inequalities that derive from injustice.

I'm just quite content to affirm that injustice is widespread, as are its effects from the past to the present. I'm not very bothered by someone saying, "Well, that has very wide implications." Yes, I agree. It has very, very wide implications for all of our institutions and all the decisions and outcomes that we see in the world.

Can you expand on the previous point contrasting the individual, rationalist, chooser and someone in need of being positively empowered by rights?

Individual choice is a worthy conception of freedom, but I think it can miss some of the ways in which people are unable to exercise their autonomy as human beings to fulfill the things that matter most to their lives and to achieve basic functionings.

It's great to talk about being able to choose what school your child goes to, for instance. But people often are fearful even of having their children go to school because of checks by immigration authorities. Even the basic ability to just navigate the world physically, without feeling fear. There's a lot of discussion about why ethnic minorities tend to live in certain neighborhoods. That too, I think is about maybe the most basic right, which is the right to life and security, and racism is a clear threat to people's life and security.

You do not want to live in certain neighborhoods because you're fearful that you might be shouted at and beaten up. In philosophy people understand that without the right to life, none of the other rights really go anywhere. If you feel like you can't even fulfill basic security for you and your family you can hardly be said to be free.

We know that half of Black children in Britain and 54% of Pakistani children and 60% of Bangladeshi children are living in poverty in Britain today. This should not be just viewed as injustices or inequalities. It prevents people from making choices and from doing things with their lives. Those of us who have the resources to put enough food in our children's bellies, who do get enough calories, don't even have to think about that.

If conventional negative liberty is good it often doesn't capture other threats to freedom. What would a truly free state, what would a truly free Britain look like according to your ideal?
There are basic functionings that all human beings should fulfill and those go beyond the right to having food and housing, but even to things like friendship, love, leisure time. I think these are things that all human beings value and that contribute, not just to our well-being, but our sense of who we are as individuals and the value that we find in our personal identities. I would say everyone should have access to these basic functionings. (They may not always be fully fulfilled, because people might choose not to access some of them.)

We value having leisure time because it allows us to explore the things that matter in our life, beyond work and even sometimes beyond our family, to have that time for ourselves. I would even argue the possibility of love might be a basic freedom that everyone should be entitled to. Obviously some people might be more satisfied living as hermits, but I would like them to have the opportunity to be loved and have relationships and connections with others.

I think you can talk about liberty very high mindedly, but without adequate resources, without a society that dismantles discrimination, it can remain an abstract ideal. To make it real we need both enabling conditions and the removal of constraints on people fulfilling those basic functionings.

I would also point out that when we talk about constraints on freedom we are not just talking about the state. I think the libertarian right focuses too much on the state as the main source of constraint. There are other constraints; I would call racism, sexism, and homophobia constraints on people's choices. I think that's why they need to be dismantled. These prejudices are also reinforced by unjust structures; structures that deny individuals agency, choice, and liberty.

In addition to all that, we also need certain enabling conditions. We need to do more than merely remove constraints. We need to positively enable people, both through them having resources, and through them living in a different kind of society. I would suspect, for example, that one of the biggest unfreedoms is the fact that people often can't choose the labor they want, and are forced to choose crap jobs because there's no realistic alternative for them.

So there's quite a lot that would need to change in the economy in terms of enabling people as well as removing the constraints. One thing I would say about leftists who are thinking about re-envisioning the economy, they should make sure that they don't just assume that more just economic structure will be free from racial discrimination. Those two sources of unfreedom are linked, but we'll have to confront both in order to be truly free.

So in order to have a fully free society, we not only have to do redistribution, we have to do antiracism. You're in public policy, you advocate for reforms. What specifically do we need to do to make our society more free on the antidiscrimination side of the aisle?

There are tools within the existing legislative framework, but they're just not being implemented. Windrush saw that. There are things like the public sector equality duty; the basic principle is to make sure that all policies don't have intended or unintended effects that increase inequality on grounds of what in the jargon is called "protected characteristics," in this case race.

I don't think that when it came to immigration policy that the government did that properly. It followed the letter, but not the spirit of the law. Similarly with the Treasury, I wrote a briefing and a letter to the Treasury saying that the budget was going to hit the poorest Black and Asian women hardest. The Treasury's response was that wasn't their intent. That also the hardest working people were benefiting. So not an answer to whether it was fair or right that the budget increased racial inequalities, and a little sting in the tail suggesting that the poor Black and Asian women weren't very hardworking.

Secondly, we need to better mobilize Black and Asian communities so that they are better resourced to challenge and mobilize against racism generally, but also the discriminatory policies that the state implements. Of course, that is a question of organizing among people of color, but I think it's also a question of mobilizing in white communities; all people in Britain should be better educated and mobilized.

The third thing is, I am an advocate of universal policies around the economy as well. I think what's happened with class and race is quite interesting. With race, there tends to be an antidiscrimination frame, which is focused on legal protections in the labor market, housing, and public services. That sort of legalistic approach is less focused on large-scale structural change, this frame tends to accept existing structures and just tries to make them fair or nondiscriminatory.

Around class by contrast, the focus has been on big socioeconomic reforms, or even macroeconomic change. I think both could be informed by the other approach.

How so?
In terms of race, we need to think more about the ways that our economic system and our wider organizations reproduce racial

discrimination, not just through individual intent, but just through the history and the long effects of racism in our society. It's not enough to ask, "How do we create an organization where black people better fit in?" Rather than trying to fix, or protect, the Black person, so that they're a round peg for a round hole, we need to ask why do we only have round holes? Should we not have a mix of square and round holes? Why have the holes been crafted to exclude some people but not others?

In terms of class, I think one of the things that's emerged with Brexit is the left is very comfortable talking about class in terms of material interests and macroeconomic performance. They're less good about talking about the experience of class, which is actually often quite like race in terms of feeling humiliated and discriminated against, in virtue of your accent, in virtue of which school you went to.

You've talked a lot about structural change. Should we also work on changing attitudes or do you think change in discriminatory beliefs will follow a change in discriminatory structures?

I think it's circular actually, especially with discrimination. So one reason why attitudes persist is because the inequalities persist. People then see that Black people have worse outcomes and, unlike you and me, a lot of people think that means they are like less hardworking, less intelligent, or less worthy. So the ongoing existence of inequalities then become a justification for the attitudes.

But the attitudes are, as I said before, almost freestanding and they do need tackling on their own terms. That's one reason why, in my career, I am focused on school curriculum. That's obviously only getting at young people but it's part of the long-term solution.

The other place for action, which is extremely challenging, is how we talk about who we are as a society, or as a country. Conversations that get at things like Britishness and belonging. If you can talk in terms of belonging, that would be my route in, because I think people need to feel like they belong to something more than themselves. They find value and meaning in the communities they belong to, they have particular local connections with neighbors and friends who help them with childcare, with particular schools and teachers, not the education system generally or abstractly. Those are communities that have their own logic and meaning.

In multicultural cities, you can often be quite successful in talking about belonging in a way that is pluralistic and tolerant. There are lots of places where the community has changed slightly but everybody is comfortable and is positive about it. Even there, however, you still need to proactively to talk about the benefits and the contributions of diversity. Not just passively hope that tolerance will win out through generational change. That's one of the things that much of the left messed up on, and one of the reasons why even Brexit, to an extent, happened.

Under New Labour in particular, there was an assumption that just talking about "Cool Britannia" in a very hand-wavy way would be sufficient. That older attitudes would die off by themselves and everybody would embrace pluralism without the positive case for it having to be made.

That said, the hand-wavy stuff was, for all its ills, better than what we have now.

I think liberals over the last few decades assumed that the fundamental questions of nondiscrimination and the benefits of multiculturalism had been essentially won. That overt racists were a tiny fringe minority. That left them really ill-equipped to have a conversation regarding Trump, regarding some of the more racist motivations for Brexit, because they assumed they didn't need to have that discussion anymore.

I absolutely think that's right. You see that in the policy framing of racism as being an issue of extremism on the far right. So it's very much a niche thing that we can keep over there. It's not part of our mainstream. It hasn't infected the body politic. It doesn't look like housing policy, it looks like street thugs from the EDL beating up people.

If you have a conception of racism as extremism, I think that's, first of all, to misunderstand what racism is. Racism is a structural phenomenon that has deep roots in our society and that all of us can actually accidentally pick up. If you think that there's no racism in your tradition, be you left, liberal, centrist, or conservative, you just don't know your tradition very well in my view. It also leaves you, as you say, very ill-equipped to deal with it.

There was always resistance to diversity, bubbling underneath, especially in the tabloids. It's both that people like Blair didn't understand the deeper origins of racism within Britain, within our institutions, within our intellectual culture, and within the sense of who we are as a people. But also, he was nervous because he thought that if you were too explicit in support for diversity, you might get a backlash. There was probably that thinking too.

In this government, by contrast, there's definitely a sense that we shouldn't be ashamed of our history, which includes statues to slavers. The Culture Secretary just announced yesterday that it's going to be made illegal to take down statues. So obviously that means that he thinks that statutes to slavers should stand for all time.

You see it with Johnson talking about how much we as a country love freedom at the same time as how we're going to restrict the liberties and freedoms of foreigners. The view seems to be that there's a universal duty for the state not to interfere, but only for British people.

This is where that issue of belonging intersects, which is the government's rhetoric looks laissez faire, but it's extremely statist and repressive when it comes to noncitizens, and when it comes to people they don't think should be citizens. It's not a universalist account of liberty, it's a nationalist one. A lot of right libertarians say they are for the liberty of everyone but they often constrain it at national borders.

Would your vision of freedom require us to move toward open borders?

Yeah, I think that's the missing piece in a lot of the freedom of movement debate. One of the failures of the European project was the limitation of freedom of movement merely as a labor freedom, because if you looked at it, most Europeans were unable to vote in the national elections of countries they moved to. If you looked at it further, not all Europeans were equally able to avail themselves of the choice to move because of issues of wealth and income.

They had no account of how the notion of free movement within Europe was going to move toward a wider notion of human freedom of movement, or even if that was their principle. So either they dodged it and it made it look like Europe was a fortress for White migrants, or they hand-waved toward it, but didn't have any practical account of how we get from here to there.

I accept it's not going to happen anytime soon, but I would like to see some steppingstones along the way to dismantling the current border regime. One thought is we should introduce the third plank of international migration, in addition to refugee and labor migration. There should be a random allocation from the poorest countries to the richest countries every year that allows, say, 10,000 to 20,000 people from Malawi or 30,000 to 40,000 people from Kenya to move to a global wealthy country.

Borders are a big source of unfreedom, and they're very racialized. I think that's another thing we don't spot; we spot that the state constrains our liberty by imposing taxes on us, but we don't spot that the state constrains people's liberty by preventing you from moving from country A to country B, unless you have the right passport.

The argument that global freedom of movement would increase freedom seems a fairly straightforward one: Freedom entails choosing your life plans, people would be more able to do that without immigration restrictions.
Though I think many people would say there would be significant adverse consequences.

Yeah, people on the left would say that's a libertarian argument about choice. On the left, we care about community, and that's going to erode our communities. I know that that's the response because I've heard that response. There's a communitarian streak in laborism, which is very strong in Britain.

They would argue one of the reasons Brexit happened is there was too much change in places like Mansfield. The sense of who they were was being eroded by immigration, and the benefits of mass migration don't flow to working-class people in England. People aren't just units to move around the world as either labor market contributors or welfare maximizers, they have values, traditions, communities, and identities to which they belong. There's a communitarian streak in laborism, which is very strong in Britain.

To which you would say what?
To which I would say of course, community matters, but why define community in such a static way? Communities change all the time and the static vision can have its own problems: for instance, an idealized account of working-class history and identity as wound up in manufacturing jobs excludes many other people—women disabled people, LGBT people.

I think what's also happened is people bought into this notion that only elites like multiculturalism, that it's about like going to lots of fancy, expensive, different restaurants or whatever.

Whereas I actually think if you look at the history, working-class people have been quite happy to interact with people of other working-class backgrounds. In fact, arguably more so. If you look at the Lancaster cotton mills in the 1860s—that they chose to starve rather than take slave cotton. Even though none of them had ever left Lancaster, none of them were educated beyond the age of sixteen, they saw the need for solidarity.

To conclude, how do we, as campaigners, sell our vision better? We've discussed what you think a truly free society would look

like, how do you message that to people who might not agree on every issue?

There's definitely a principled case for considering racism as a liberty issue. I think there's also a pragmatic case in that it foregrounds its impacts on actual people: Racism is a constraint on people's lives, the choices they want to make. Racism means that they can't make basic choices about where to live, what schools they can send their children to, and what jobs are available to them.

Even the more high-minded ideals about human flourishing can make for effective political communication: I would like to be able to be able to set out the kind of life I want to live. Racism is a barrier to that.

The other thing that helps people understand this, from a messaging point of view, is when people see cases of Black people being treated unfairly, or in ways constraining their liberty. George Floyd obviously is the most egregious case of liberty being constrained; being murdered because of your race. But also in the Windrush case people suddenly saw, "Oh my God, it's something that really affects people's lives." People who lived in this country for decades were put in detention centers. People were denied access to healthcare. People were deported to countries they hadn't seen since they were children. People were forcibly put in planes by the state because of racial discrimination.

Seeing those individual cases made a difference. The vast majority of the British public thought what was happening was terrible. It wasn't just leftists. Not only that, but they saw it was a systemic issue. They didn't think it was a one-off. There was a litany of people coming forward. They all shared certain circumstances, and their experience was all very similar. In a way, you almost didn't need to explain it.

Some on the left may see that type of messaging as too individualistic. Ultimately, though, we're not just aiming for a systematic change because we like good societies. We want good societies because we think the people who live in those societies will be living better lives. What matters is human beings and the lives that they're living. We shouldn't fetishize a Marxist or socialist paradise. What we want is individuals to be living in a paradise because we want them to be happy and flourishing.

In the end, when structural equality is the norm, when we eliminate racism and sexism and homophobia, what we'll have left is human beings and their individual personalities and worth. We should aim for that end. We should be not shy of saying, "We want to have a world in which every human being who lives on this planet has the ability to make choices free from constraints, not worrying about basic needs. Where they are also able to pursue the more ephemeral bits of being a human, like loving others, caring for others, exploring human knowledge, whether that's philosophy, history, art, craft, or athletics." To achieve that aim, to realize human liberty, we must tackle racism.

Further Reading

Bridget Byrne, Claire Alexander, Omar Khan, James Nazroo, and William Shankley. *Ethnicity, Race and Inequality in the UK: State of the Nation.* Bristol University Press 2020.

Gentleman, Amelia. *The Windrush Betrayal: Exposing the Hostile Environment.* Guardian Faber Publishing 2019.

Olusoga, David. *Black and British: A Forgotten History*. Pan 2017.

For more information on the Runnymede Trust, as well as reports and resources: runnymedetrust.org.

10

Defending EU Liberalism

Ian Dunt

Twitter is hardly known as an area for sophisticated, detailed political analysis. Even before the Trump presidency the platform was basically synonymous with angry, unpleasant, and uninformed discourse. To every rule there is an exception, however. Like many during the Brexit debate, I found Ian Dunt through his exceptional real-time Twitter reporting of parliamentary debates. Funny, often angry, but also sharp, knowledgeable, and rooted in the facts of the case, he was an invaluable guide through some of the most perplexing moments in British political history.

When I got Ian on the podcast, I pushed him to give an account of the values that underlined his pro-Remain politics—as it turns out, he had been working on a book on just that. This conversation starts by looking at the nature of liberalism. Ian argues strongly for a liberalism centered on "the greatest freedom for the greatest number." We consider the history of liberalism and offer various ideas for why it (seems to be) losing ground in current European politics. Specifically, we discuss how liberalism has lost the ability to engage in popular discourse to defend itself and how liberal arguments have taken place in the courtroom, or in journals, not on the streets or front pages. We consider the various normative complexities of Brexit, and Ian ends with a call for the defense of the liberal order.

Ian Dunt is a journalist based in London. He edits the website Politics.co.uk from the Houses of Parliament and contributes regularly to a variety of newspapers and magazines, including

Ian Dunt, *Defending EU Liberalism* In: *What is Freedom?*. Edited by: Toby Buckle, Oxford University Press.
© Oxford University Press 2021. DOI: 10.1093/oso/9780197572214.003.0011

the *Guardian*, the *Irish Times*, the *Washington Post*, and *Prospect*. He is one of the hosts on the hit podcast *Remainiacs*, and his new show *The Bunker*. He is a prolific media commentator, appearing regularly on Sky News, the BBC, al-Jazeera, and many others.

His best-selling first book, *Brexit: What the Hell Happens Now*, first laid bare the realities of Britain's exit from Europe. The public paid for it to be sent to every MP in the House of Commons. He writes primarily about Brexit, nationalism, free speech, immigration, drug policy, and criminal justice. His new book, *How to Be a Liberal*, came out in 2020 to much acclaim.

You describe yourself as a liberal journalist. Could you start by saying what liberalism means to you?
Liberalism is extremely broad, and there's no agreement whatsoever on what it is. For me, liberalism is the attempt to establish the greatest quality and quantity of freedom for the greatest number of people.

There's an awful lot involved in just making that statement. We are dealing with a political philosophy that is based on the individual, the individual as the primary unit of politics. Reason is also completely tied up with the birth of liberalism. You can't really separate reason from liberalism. They were born together and they die together.

There's also something broader, I think, which is that it's the kind of political philosophy that requires you to make day-to-day judgments. It's a nontribal judgment. You don't get to appeal to some kind of utopia on the top end, as, for instance, communists do. You are forced to make day-to-day judgments, assessing relative levels of freedom for people. It can be fairly superficial things, like a smoking ban, or it can be much, much more deep-seated, like the rights of individuals when they are a protected minority group. It requires that kind of day-to-day thinking. And that kind of day-to-day thinking has never been popular because it provides no easy answers.

You have to keep on making these judgements for yourself. You don't get to say that a leader will do it for you. There's no political philosopher to do that for you. You have to make the judgment. But that's also, of course, what makes it beautiful because it makes it the most instinctively rebellious political philosophy. It cannot be anything but a challenge to power because it places the ability to reason, to make those judgments, with the individual. It can never help a power structure because it always centers on the individual to make their own judgments.

On the American left, "liberal" is increasingly becoming a bit of a dirty word to mean centrist, someone who's insufficiently committed to egalitarianism or social justice.
It sounds like you view liberalism as, dare I say, the original bad boy of ideologies.

Thank you, I'm going to steal that.

To be honest, the way that we in Britain use the word "liberal" is exactly the same as the way that it's being used in America right now, in terms of the public debate. That's unusual because, historically, America has used the word "liberalism" in a completely different way to the way it's been used in Europe. For years in America it usually just meant "lefty."

Right now, we're pretty much where you are: The right hates liberalism, because it tends to suggest multiculturalism and openness toward immigration. The left tends to hate it because they think of it as this sort of Blairist, centrist, neoliberal idea of not interfering with the market that just doesn't care enough about marginalized groups or poor people.

I think there's a couple of aspects to how liberals became so alienated from both left and right. The first thing to mention there is that liberalism does not have a set view on economics. This has been its greatest strength and its greatest weakness. The reason it doesn't have a set view is because it is quite difficult to come up with one idea of how the liberal function of the expansion of freedom operates when it comes to property rights.

That was there 400 years ago; it was right there from the very beginning. And it's there now. Do you, for instance, say that when someone earns money they have complete control over that money? Does freedom mean that the government has no right to take any of it?

Or do you say that actually by the government taking some of that money and, for instance, creating street lighting or creating schools, that it actually expands freedom to a much greater degree? That conflict obviously became extremely severe with the disputes between Keynes and Hayek in the 20th century. Once you get the Hayekian victory, through pretty much all of my lifetime—certainly throughout the eighties and nineties—most liberals gave up any kind of really critical economic thinking during that time.

For a long time there was just a sense that the economic fight is done; the free market is simply more efficient than anything the state will ever do, in almost any area. Liberal thinking people were privatizing pretty much anything that moves and some of what they were privatizing were frankly insane things to have in private hands.

There was a point where we privatized probation! If anyone can show me how you properly make a profit off that I am all ears. But they have never been able to demonstrate it because, most of the time, when you take someone that's out of jail, you've got someone who has a variety of mental health problems. They usually have very low literacy rates. They have often, for pretty much their entire lifetime, not been able to solve conflicts or disputes without the use of violence. They often live in hard to reach areas without decent family and friendship connections and without career prospects.

There simply isn't a profit motive to get private companies involved in this. It does not work. And yet because of the success of Hayekian ideology, even that kind of deranged prospect was implemented. Liberalism basically stopped being able to make the case for saying that it was radical because it gave up on the economic side of the argument.

From the Beveridge report back to, I would argue, John Stuart Mill, there's a long tradition of liberalism having a much more expansive conception of freedom than the libertarian one.
Do you think that conception of freedom is a better reading of the classical liberal tradition (which is more commonly claimed by the right)? If so, is that something we should be trying to go back to, or, in light of the ascendancy of the libertarian conception, do we need to move on to other values to ground our politics?

I absolutely would go with the former. I'm essentially an extremist liberal. There will never be a greater answer than the very simple premise of the expansion of freedom for the individual.

When you look at someone like Mill, it is laughable to me that someone would consider John Stuart Mill to be anything like neoliberal. John Stuart Mill believed in the nationalization of all land, except very small houses and gardens. He wanted an end to inheritance. He was open to nationalization of several kinds of utility. He must have looked like an alien to most of the people in Victorian times for what he believed. He was an avowed antiracist, and he was arguably Britain's first prominent male feminist.

He was of course problematic. His views on imperialism would have been quite usual for the liberal left at that time, but are of course far too complacent about empire for people today. But if you were to take any kind of generous assessment of where people's heads would have been at the time, I don't think he comes out of it that badly.

The crucial material to look at for me is *The Principles of Political Economy*. He wrote it first basically like a classical Adam Smith text. Mill is someone who Ricardo would visit when he was being brought up. (John Stuart Mill was brought up by his insane utilitarian father in what was basically a prolonged series of childhood abuse incidents.) So initially it is a pretty standard piece of classical economics.

Then Harriet Taylor, his wife, who I think is criminally underrated in liberal theory, starts working with him on a chapter on the condition of the working classes. In that chapter, in the second and third editions of the book, the socialist version of Mill comes in. He calls himself a socialist in this period. He's not using that word in the way that we would. He's talking about the creation of workers' collectives to operate within the free market.

Most importantly, he asserts the basic maxim of egalitarian liberalism: That the question of the state versus the market "does not admit of a universal solution." So we're back to the case-by-case. It's an argument that rejects the communist view that the state should do everything but equally rejects the laissez-faire view that the market should do everything. Mill's point is: What is it you are trying to do? Then let's think about what's the best way to do that. Are you making children's toys? Probably the market should do that, so that we can assess relative demand? Are you building canals or providing electricity? Probably the state should do that, so that we can avoid a private monopoly.

This is a man who basically outlined left-wing liberalism. The fact that now he is considered neoliberal, I just find the most laughable misreading of his philosophy.

The other way in which Mill is claimed by the right is by these really trivial freedom of speech guys. People who say "the clash of ideas" and "I hate safe spaces" and all of that. They'll talk about these ideas and they'll cite him. However, they have only taken half of what he had to say about free speech. First of all, comes opposition. What he demands from you is a considerable degree of confidence, and an inner steel—to go up against, not just any argument that counters yours, but the most powerful argument that counters yours, the best-constructed argument, and take it on.

Then there's a second part. And the second part is synthesis. He was obsessed with the idea of half truth in an opponent's arguments.

There will be either a lot, or even a tiny amount, of truth in there somewhere. It's your job, not just to oppose (he hated tribal animosity, especially among academics). What he looked for was an openness to sympathize enough with the opponent to find some substructure of truth in what they were saying.

One reason Mill gave for exposing your ideas to the strongest counterarguments is that if they're not actively challenged they cease to be a "living truth" and become a "dead dogma."
That seems to capture the position of current liberalism quite nicely: Before Brexit (or Trump) the arguments given for liberalism were quite anemic; the EU was half-heartedly defended as a boring necessity. Only when people recognized that liberalism was really in danger did you get these very impassioned, forceful arguments for remaining in Europe, and for a set of liberal ideals that, rightly or wrongly, the EU was felt to embody. They went from dead dogmas to living truths.

That's exactly what took place, for a variety of reasons. The first one was social liberalism; people for a long time in this country didn't really bother making the arguments for social liberalism at all, because that argument was considered won. In the same way that the free-market argument had been considered won from the 1980s onward.

In both cases, you only need to look at polls to see how naive that was.

How completely wrong that was. This was something that was happening in the political class rather than something in the country.

Something happened to liberals in that capacity, too. Not only did they stop bothering to make the arguments, but when they did make the argument, they made it in court. The European convention of human rights, for example, is an extremely powerful piece of law. One of the most beautiful liberal accomplishments of the postwar period for me. This, along with other accomplishments like freedom of movement, allowed all of these fights to take place in a courtroom. As soon as you say, "we're going to defend this immigrant being targeted by the state," you will often be able to find a right to family life, or a right to privacy, or something that you can use to protect them. Or you could use judicial review in lots of these cases in order to challenge a piece of legislation, or a piece of government policy, that seems authoritarian. But that's where those fights took place; in courtrooms.

They weren't taking place in town halls. They weren't even really taking place in newspapers or on TV. The liberal fight went to the top level and they forgot how to have normal conversations. So then the referendum happens and these chancing scumbags come along and just start spewing lies, reactionary lies, fundamentally objectively wrong statements about how trade policy works, or what the law is. Then you've got all these experts who are left destroyed by what it's like to argue with someone who is prepared to engage in that way. What they do is the much more genteel, respectable world of the courtroom, or possibly the broadsheets, at most. And we got our arses handed to us.

Now on the post side of it, suddenly you see something completely different. You see people explicitly and repeatedly identifying themselves with liberal ideas. Now these are all Remainers, these are all people that see it through the EU. But when they talk about things, they're talking about being open to immigration, open to having various ideas in your head at the same time, open to international institutions as a way of controlling the power of the nation-state. If there's any good side to what is taking place, it's exactly, as you say, this stuff is coming alive. People have an identity in relation to it, instead of it being something that's unchallenged and assumed, it is becoming something explicit and best of all, very aggressive.

Mill also asks us to try and see the truth in the opposing argument. What is there for liberals to learn from the Brexit vote? If

nothing else, surely the fact that the EU couldn't justify liberal values in a way that could secure democratic consent speaks to a huge weakness on the part of European liberalism.

The trouble is trying to separate out the intellectual core of the Brexit argument from self-interested, day-to-day political point scoring. You would expect me to say this, but actually it's quite hard to find the intellectual core—to find people that are consistent about what it is that they're arguing in their euroskepticism. I use the word "euroskepticism" pointedly because euroskepticism has a tremendous amount to recommend it. In fact, I think it's central to any effective functioning of the European project.

Just what does Europe involve? Europe is born in the ashes of the Second World War. It's basically France and Germany saying, look, we've done this twice. The third time there's a really good chance there's going to be nothing left. So, how do we do it? Their answer is a liberal answer, which is to say that trade replaces war. That you get through trade what you otherwise would through war. And so they started to meld economies together.

Now that project is massive. It's the most advanced and sophisticated trade project in the history of mankind. It absolutely involves getting rid of tariffs, but much more deeply than that it involves harmonizing regulations: This is always the great obstacle to trade. If you've got one country that says, "we're going to have this mixture of noble gases in car headlights," or "we're only going to have these chemicals allowed in children's toys," or "we're going to have this process for creating meat to make sure that it's as humane as possible," as soon as you make that domestic political decision, that legal decision, you have to check on the border for the stuff that's coming in. That creates blockages, and that prevents trade. The European union response is, "we'll just all have the same regulations." Now that puts this rocket fuel into trade. It's done tremendous things for Britain. Britain was the poor man of Europe in the seventies.

This is basically unheard of, but there's a flip side to that, and there's no point pretending otherwise. It's that you're giving up sovereignty. It seems to me that sovereignty in these areas is not really that important. I mean, do I really care where the regulations are made on the relative noise levels of lawn mowers? And the truth is I don't. I couldn't give a fuck.

But actually lots and lots of people do. Remainers during that campaign would scoff at the idea that the word "sovereignty" would be one that would be readily picked up by the public. They thought it would sound a bit posh, a bit academic, or whatever.

But of course when you say to the public "where do you think we should make our decisions? Do you think we should make our decisions for ourselves? Or do you think that Europeans should make them?" The public feels very strongly that we should make our decisions for ourselves. That argument is not a poor one. And more than that, I do think that if you're involved in a project that is centralizing power, not just from the local level up to the, nation-state, but from countries up to a multinational institution, you need to be pretty vigilant about exactly what powers you're pushing up, exactly how you're doing it, and what your democratic structure is to assess them. The EU has not been good at that. It would be much better if there was some recognition of the fact that it needs to radically improve.

However, I do have to point one thing out. Which is that despite that, the referendum campaign was not lost on the basis of sovereignty, it was lost on the basis of immigration. That argument is a very different argument. It's much harder for me to see truth in it because I think it stems from a dangerous, quite poisonous place. I think it needs to be countered wherever we find it.

It's not just what powers go to what level. When it comes to Europe, liberals often talk as if they wish they could do away with democracy altogether; that the EU shouldn't have to justify itself to the electorate, or secure the consent of the governed.

"Constitutional change should not be decided by plebiscite" was a common refrain after the referendum. But how else should it be done? Are we to have it simply mandated by elite consensus?

I don't say that, as I don't think it's helpful. I know the kind of cultural background when people talk that way is perceived as a kind of sneering superiority. However, I definitely am not a fan of referendums anymore. I think you'd be very hard pressed to look at the way that we are discussing these matters right now, and think that anything healthy is coming from the debate.

The reality is that these are tremendously complicated issues and you can take aspects of them and hold votes. That potentially might work. But when you're trying to talk about forty years of systemwide legal cooperation that affects things like security, animal rights, the way in which your industry and your economy is structured, it's just not the case that any of that was understood. It wasn't even understood by the Remain side, let alone by the Leave side.

So what happened is they held a referendum where people wanted to say, "I don't like the establishment" (which is a word that you hear a lot, but no one's ever able to tell you exactly what that means) and "I don't like David Cameron, so I'm gonna give him a kicking." The cumulative effect of that, people have been aghast to learn, is one of the most fiendishly complicated generation-defining issues they could imagine. On that basis, I have to say it definitely doesn't feel like this has been a very good way to do things. However, there is an issue on the lack of consent in the European project.

I think you're fundamentally right in a couple of ways. First of all, almost any time you get people to vote on this, they vote against it. The French did, the Dutch did, the Irish did, and now the Brits have done it. (In those other three cases, they asked again until people changed their mind. And that was on the Lisbon treaty, not quite on in-or-out membership.) So we still seem to keep on getting this result. We also have voter turnout levels during European elections, which are usually around 30%–40% in countries where you get over 50% on a general election vote. That suggests that there is a consent problem here.

It's not a done deal, though. On the other side, you find that most people in most countries do want to Remain. Most people do feel European and support the European Union project. There is a system in place that offers quite a decent degree of scrutiny. I would say the European system is good on scrutiny of legislation. What it's bad at is exactly where did this legislation originate from? Mostly it originates from the council (which is elected heads of state) and then the commission (which is sort of its civil service, it's also shady as fuck, frankly).

Then there's the softer point of how the EU conducts itself. No one in their right mind would ever watch a debate in the European Union because it's so powerfully dull. There's none of the structure of scrutiny that actually encourages popular investment in it. They've been really bad at that. That's because it is ultimately a trade project with these other trappings underneath. So it's particularly vulnerable to becoming very technocratic and quite aloof from the public.

That's the big failing right? A lot of the mechanisms we have to protect liberal freedoms are embedded in a complex project. Worse still, the defenders of that project often seem to have given up trying to explain it to a regular person.

I really have very little sympathy for them; if they don't even try to make their case they can't be surprised when people don't buy it.

A part of that is intellectual bravery on the part of liberals. And the other part is communication skills. Now what has happened to communication skills? Tony Blair, for example, when he's running for power, he's got the left with him. He needs to win over enough of the right. And the slogan that he uses for crime is "tough on crime, tough on the causes of crime." Now, mate, that's genius.

You pretty much had something for everyone, but it has a structure. There's intellectual content there. As it turned out, he didn't deliver on it; he mostly put home secretaries in charge that were fire and brimstone people in order to keep the rightwing press. But just in terms of how do you make the argument? That's very, very effective. That you have to address the underlying systematic economic causes of crime, but if someone mugs you we'll put them in jail. We'll try to stop there being more muggers in the world. We'll put more money into it. But at the point that someone does mug you, they're still gonna get the fire and brimstone. That was very effective.

This stuff can be done. What it needs is for people to think there is a democratic mandate to communicate simply. That's not just for politicians or intellectuals, it's also for journalists. Journalists have really given up on their job and my God, you saw it during the Brexit debate. As soon as the word "tariff" came up you see fear in the producers' eyes because they think they're losing the audience by the second. There's no attempt by journalists to try to explain very simply what this stuff is. I mean, tariffs—it's so easy. It's just taxes on goods when they go over a border. That's all it is. There is no one on this planet who cannot understand the concept of what a tariff is.

But producers have this terror that once you go into any degree of complexity, you will lose your audience. And so what kind of political coverage do you get? You get political soap opera. It's really a betrayal of voters because it doesn't hand them the tools with which to form independent judgements about what is going on in the world around them. So it's not just politicians. I have to say my own guys, journalists have been having an absolutely fucking dreadful time doing their jobs, and the standard has been poor.

What would have been wrong with accepting the result of the referendum, leaving the EU, but retaining all of the trade agreements and freedom of movement?
There's nothing wrong with that in theory. In fact, I wrote a book called *Brexit, What the Hell Happens Now?* which essentially

recommended exactly that path: to stay in the single market, stay in the customs union and leave the European union, which is basically as soft an exit as you can implement.

That seems to me the moral response to a 48% to 52% result. It's doubly the case because between 20% to 40% of leave voters were either pro-immigration, or would not be prepared to see any risk to the economy from limiting immigration. So leaving the single market, or ending freedom of movement doesn't actually have a proper mandate from the result.

So, I quite liked the look of the Norway option, and I even think it would have been possible to make it work. Although it's a humiliating position for a country of Britain's size to be in, because you are going to take regulations that you didn't even have a say in.

But that's the nature of a compromise. Everyone's a bit unhappy.

Agreed. But it isn't great, and it's just not where we are right now. Let's be honest. It's not a debate about tariffs. It's not about trade. It's not about any of that. It's about identity. That's what the Brexit debate is about. It's a culture war about identity. Do you want a closed country? Do you have a pure idea of your national culture where you don't have to work with others or take on immigrants? Or do you have an open, more cosmopolitan view that is open to a variety of ideas and a variety of people? That's what Brexit's actually about. And in that context, it very quickly turned into this insane, tribal dogfight.

What's been so interesting is the degree to which people were willing to sacrifice other things they claimed to care about for the vision (some would say fantasy) of a closed society. I remember a poll where a majority of Conservative Party members thought Northern Ireland and Scotland leaving the Union would be a price worth paying for Brexit.

That poll was one of the most startling and depressing things that I'd seen in a long time, because it's basically people going completely mad. You're saying "I believe in this thing so much I'm willing to see the breakup of my country and everyone made poorer." It's an extraordinary place to be. It's essentially a form of extremism.

Ultimately, with the caveats in place that we mentioned about the faults of the EU, the fight that we're having right now is a fight for liberalism. This is evident when you have an argument with people who are simply not dealing in objective fact. There has been an erosion of the idea of truth. The phrase "will of the people" is used over the idea of individuals and what people are essentially representing is a phrase that is used commonly now: "the white working class." An extremely troubling way of saying "over here is proper Britain, and over there, they're not really proper Britons." The approach toward immigration, which I would say is part and parcel of a standard attack on minorities, we've seen throughout history—toward Catholics, toward Jewish people, toward gay people, toward Kulaks. The attack on international institutions that Trump has embarked on with the WTO and with the UN is similar to the Brexiters against the EU. These are quite conscious attacks on liberalism and the defense against them is a defense of basic liberal values.

We are basically having a political philosophy fight in the most vigorous terms imaginable. This is a real crunch point for the kind of future that we're going to live in. It's important to actually have the fight, to make the case. You've got to do the Tony Blair thing; you've got to win the argument. It's not complicated. You've just got to win the argument. And that's the battle we're in right now.

Further Reading

Dunt, Ian. *Brexit: What the Hell Happens Now?* Canbury Press 2016.
Dunt, Ian. *How to Be a Liberal: The Story of Liberalism and the Fight for Its Life.* Canbury Press 2020.

11

Civil Rights Activism

Mary Frances Berry

One topic that is often neglected in works on freedom is what life is like for those on the ground fighting for it, when are they effective, and why. Making activism a core part of your life is not always easy. It can be both exhilarating and deeply meaningful, but it can also be exhausting and depressing. All of us who do this work experience moments of burnout from either personal fatigue or political failures.

In such moments it's worth taking a step back and taking stock. History is a natural place to look to here: how did those who came before you handle setbacks? How did they keep themselves motivated? What lessons do they have for us on how to make movement work effective?

I seriously doubt there is anyone better placed to guide us through that history than Mary Frances Berry. As a member of the US Commission on Civil Rights from 1980 to 2004, and Chair from 1993 to 2004, she has been at the heart of struggles for freedom in America. She also has extensive experience in government: Between 1977 and 1980, Dr. Berry served as the Assistant Secretary for Education in the US Department of Health, Education, and Welfare (HEW). She has also served as Provost of the University of Maryland and Chancellor of the University of Colorado at Boulder.

In addition, Professor Berry is a distinguished academic historian—she has been a Geraldine R. Segal Professor of American Social Thought and Professor of History since 1987. She is the

Mary Frances Berry, *Civil Rights Activism* In: *What is Freedom?*. Edited by: Toby Buckle, Oxford University Press. © Oxford University Press 2021. DOI: 10.1093/oso/9780197572214.003.0012 author of twelve books including *Five Dollars and a Pork Chop Sandwich: Vote Buying and the Corruption of Democracy* (2016); *We Are Who We Say We Are: A Black Family's Search for Home across the Atlantic World* (2014); *And Justice For All: The United States Commission on Civil Rights and the Struggle for Freedom in America* (2009); *My Face Is Black Is True: Callie House and the Struggle for Ex-Slave Reparations* (2005); *The Pig Farmer's Daughter and Other Tales of American Justice: Episodes of Racism and Sexism in the Courts from 1865 to the Present* (1999); *Black Resistance, White Law: A History of Constitutional Racism in America* (1994, orig. 1971); *Why ERA Failed: Politics, Women's Rights, and the Amending Process of the Constitution* (1986); and *Military Necessity and Civil Rights Policy: Black Citizenship and the Constitution, 1861–1868* (1977).

This conversation took place in 2018 before Trump's impeachment in the House and the 2020 election.

You were the chairwoman of the US Civil Rights Commission. Could you tell me what that role entails?
The United States Commission on Civil Rights was started by Dwight Eisenhower, a Republican president, at around the time of the Little Rock crisis and Montgomery Bus Boycott. He did it mainly in response to complaints from African and Asian nations that were coming to independence, about all the discrimination in the United States. In the struggle for the hearts and minds of men between the Soviet Union and the United States in these underdeveloped or newly emerging nations and the way their diplomats were treated when they came to the United States.

So, the Civil Rights commission is supposed to investigate civil rights abuses all over the country, subpoena witnesses, write reports and announce its findings, and to suggest remedies for the findings.

In its first years all the way up through the 1960s, most of the civil rights laws that were passed were recommended by the commission. Unlike other commissions who have reports and then they just sit on the shelf somewhere, most of the recommendations were actually implemented over the years until we got to the Reagan administration.

The idea of the commission is that it's independent of political control, but you were fired by the President Reagan, right?

You can't be fired by the president. The commission was set up by Eisenhower and approved by Congress to be an independent agency in the federal government. For people who don't really understand the system, they don't understand why we have independent agencies. There's some people, including the present administration, that don't believe we should have independent agencies, or they don't seem to. The idea is that even though the president plays a role in appointing people and the Congress plays a role in appointing people, you cannot be fired for expressing your views. You can resign if you wish, but you cannot be fired from the commission. The president can take your designation as Chair away, but he's not supposed to fire you. Although President Reagan did fire me, the court decided that he was wrong.

Do you take it as a badge of honor to have been fired by Reagan?

Oh, I think it was wonderful to be fired by him, because he told the press that he fired me because I served at his pleasure and I wasn't giving him very much pleasure. That was because I kept criticizing his policies to turn back the clock on civil rights,—as I was supposed to do. The federal district court here in DC said that you cannot fire a watchdog for biting and that by law, we were a watchdog.

I took your most recent book as a call to arms to not give up on activism in the age of Trump.

Having a big part of your life working for a freer and fairer world is often very challenging. I've seen activist burnout so many times, people coming to the point where they reach an unsustainable level of frustration and exhaustion. I feel it in myself.

(I'm just approaching about a decade working in activism, which I know is short compared to your efforts, and I'm sure my trials and tribulations are quite trivial compared to those of others.)

You're older and wiser than me and I'm wondering if you have any advice for me and people who find ourselves in this position.

Well, Toby, I think that the advice that I am about to give you can be summed by what I say in the book. What you have to do, and what I learned over the years, is you have to focus your resistance. You have to focus your reform efforts. There's so many issues to work on, because there're so many things that are wrong, but you have to pick out laser-like what it is you're going to work on and what the goal is.

If the goal is marriage equality, focus on that. If people want you to work on something else, say, "No, I'm working on marriage equality." If the goal is to get Medicare for All, say, "I'm working on Medicare for All." Whatever it is you happen to be working on.

Now, if you focus laser-like and if you simplify what it is you're working for, your goal, and stick with it, then you won't be tired. It took us a year and a half to get the law passed which made sanctions against South Africa because of apartheid. A year and a half of marches, protests, getting arrested, boycotts, and taking over buildings.

The steering committee met every day during the week at my house, that whole time, and all of us had other jobs. Then we would go out in the afternoon to a protest and our chapters in other cities would do the same thing. We did that and worked with the Congress, our Congress people who helped us to get a bill passed. Ronald Reagan was opposed to it and publicly said he was going to veto the bill even when we got it passed.

When he was inaugurated the second time, it was so cold that they canceled the inaugural parade but we were outside protesting and getting arrested with groups of people who came to get arrested. All we did that year was focus on that and even after we passed it, he vetoed the bill and then we had to go out again and get it passed over his veto, which we did.

If we had been trying to work on five things or three things and not saying, "Here's the issue, here's what we want to do," we would have been totally exhausted and probably wouldn't have been able to function.

Also, think of resistance and protest as something that gives you pleasure. I often tell people that I'm never happier than when I'm with a like-minded group of people, engaged in some kind of activity against injustice. Lou Hamer once said that if there are only three of us at the meeting when we call it, that's enough. At least we have three.

It's a high. It's not a high like smoking marijuana or something, but it's a high when you are able to work on a cause and you have people working in the cause, you've thought it out very carefully and planned it, you're organized, and you know what the goal is, and the goal is simple.

The drug analogy isn't crazy. You've got to try and go back to find that original high again and again when it can just become just work and just tiring.

You know what else, Toby? What you do in a movement is to think of different strategies. Don't keep doing the same thing over and over again. When you think about the AIDS crisis, for example and the focus to get AZT at a price that people could afford when it was made available. It was an effort to get Ronald Reagan to talk about the AIDS crisis, he wouldn't even mention it until Rock Hudson died (because Rock Hudson was one of his friends). Before that, you couldn't get him to say anything.

Well, when ACT UP started its guerrilla activities, they didn't do the same thing every single time they went out. They would try different tactics. I remember the time they came to the commission meeting in their costumes and sat in the audience at the public meeting and then turned their backs on the commission, which got great press. They did that because we had two members who had said awful things about the AIDS crisis and about gay people.

They would try to think of different things to do, so they kept media attention. If you don't have media attention, then you haven't done anything because nobody will know what you did, and what you want to do is grow your movement.

If they had just gone out every day and done exactly the same thing, I'm sure they would've been exhausted and bored and they wouldn't have gotten the attention.

Trump's victory was a catalyst for many people feeling a sense of defeat. Personally I wasn't as surprised as some and, if anything, it marginally increased my motivation. Many other people just looked at that and thought, "what's the point?'

One of the reasons why I wrote the book is because right after the election I had some speaking engagements already scheduled. I went to a state where there were women's organizations, state agencies that deal with women's rights. They were having a convention and I was to give a keynote speech. That was scheduled a long time before and at the time everybody there thought that Hillary Clinton was going to be elected and the event was calendared shortly after the election, so they were going to have a great celebration.

I was going to talk about that and when I got there, they said, "Well, first of all, could we have dinner with the heads of these various organizations?" Could I have dinner and listen to what they had to say? I went in and they spent hours telling me how awful they felt, how they were in mourning and then finally, some of them cried and wanted to wallow, I thought, in this feeling of despair and I'm not a despairing person.

It was exactly the same when I came into work that day. It was like a funeral.

People were mourning. So the next day when I got ready to speak, I said mourning is fine. You can do that for a little while, but do what my mother always says which is when you're concerned about something, get up off your "do nothing" stool and do something. What you ought to do is figure out what you're going to do.

When I came back home, I got several emails from my editor, who said, "You know what? You need to write a book about your experience with resistance based on your research and your experience to tell people what you can do about making change and how to organize, not just the nuts and bolts of it, but a narrative about how these things happen so people can figure out better what lessons they can learn."

I'm a historian and, while it doesn't teach us everything, we do learn something from history, because human beings are the same no matter which time you live in. There's greed, there's envy, jealousy, all the different aspects of the human condition. I thought about it. I didn't want to write the book because I figured I'd written too many books and I just finished the year before writing another one.

But after talking to and listening to people, I decided I would write it, that book became *History Teaches Us to Resist*. The purpose was to show that there is always something you can do. It's not enough to just say, "I don't like Trump," or, "I hate Trump," over and over and over again. It's tempting to go up to people who are Trump administrators sitting in a restaurant and tell them off and tell them to leave. Probably if I walked into a restaurant and I saw one, I may do the same thing. But I know that's not really resistance because all that'll happen is somebody else will replace them.

If Trump left, you'd have Pence. That's not really the answer. It's about policy. What I wanted to do was to write about how you change policy if the president is somebody who is politically unfriendly. Also to point out to people that sometimes you can have friendly presidents, politically, but on the issues you're concerned about, they're unfavorable. That is why that historical chapter is in there about what happened with Franklin Roosevelt. He was considered a friendly president but leverage had to be used against him to get him to do something.

Bill Clinton was a "friendly" president. I called him an adaptable president. But Bill Clinton had to be pushed and Bill Clinton was terrible on gay issues and a lot of other things. I think that the lesson is that you can resist. There are ways to do it, but you have to focus and not all people who are in movements focus, and not all people who hate Trump focus on an issue.

If you're really interested in the environment or EPA, go down to the EPA and organize something. Work with the civil servants there who are often disaffected and hate what's going on. Get information and interfere with the things that they're doing. It's not enough to just hate Trump or Pruitt, Betsy DeVos, or the education department. So what? Have some kind of targeted protest against these things.

You mentioned Clinton, you described him as a "C to C+" on civil rights, can you explain?
You have to keep in mind that Clinton perpetuated the Black predator trope, which is part of the mass incarceration which has taken place in this country. Michelle Alexander writes about it in *The New Jim Crow*. That, in fact, has all these Black and Latino people in prison for minor drug offenses and other kinds of stuff and destroys families. Mass incarceration is family separation, and Clinton did that politically to show he wasn't soft on crime.

He refused to issue a stern edict against racial profiling when there were lots of people getting arrested on the streets and other places for doing nothing. Which still happens, of course. We still have Black people arrested for doing nothing except standing while Black or being a firefighter while Black or drinking a cup of coffee while Black or not drinking a cup of coffee while Black. I and others tried to get him to issue a strong edict against racial profiling, but that superpredator thing was one of the worst.

That all sounds like an F, but your ultimate verdict on Clinton was a C. Is there a positive side?
I said I would give him a C or a C+. He appointed a lot of Black people who were good, to jobs in the government. Doesn't matter they were Black. They were good. A lot of women were appointed to jobs in the administration and some gay people, and he had the first gay ambassador, Jim Hormel. He had some policies that made sense. His ending welfare as we know it, like his crime superpredator thing, were all done to show that he was a new Democrat and he could be just as conservative, as the language went in those days, as the Republicans.

I like Bill Clinton. I've always liked him, and I knew him slightly before he was president. I think he overall meant well, but he thought the Democratic Party needed to be picked up so it could get back in office and that there were certain things that needed to be done to make the party credible to a great swath of voters.

The president Trump has been compared to the most, and whose example he himself seems to have in mind, is Nixon. How would you compare the two?
Nixon had more political experience than Trump. That's the first thing. He was not an alien in a political environment in the way that Trump is; he doesn't even understand the language or anything else. He also was very egotistical like Trump. They both are very egotistical people, narcissistic and all the rest of it.

Nixon had two sides. He did some things in domestic policy that were not all bad, like he had a welfare reform proposal that wasn't too bad at the time. It didn't pass, but he had one. He let his labor department issue an affirmative action order for the construction industry, called the Philadelphia Plan, that Art Fletcher, who was assistant secretary, was responsible for. He was a wonderful Black guy.

But when the labor unions, the construction unions said they weren't going to support Nixon anymore, he abandoned it after that. He made some forays in the domestic arena that seemed promising, but he was basically hypocritical and it's true that he was a crook. He said, "I'm not a crook," but he was a crook.

What he did was in order to get elected in '68, he monkeywrenched the peace process. We in the antiwar movement had thought we had failed in ending the war. We got Johnson. Johnson resigned, but then peace didn't come and the draft was still in place and people were dying.

That's when the Weathermen formed and started engaging in violent activities. They thought we'd failed. I was depressed for years. I thought we'd totally failed and the war went on for years and people were dying. We found out that Nixon had in fact, "monkeywrenched" as he put it, the peace process. He had sent his emissaries, H. R. Haldeman was one of them, to tell the North Vietnamese not to come to the peace table that was set up.

There was a peace conference set up, and they were willing to come, but he told them, "I'll give you a better deal. Just wait. Don't come to the peace table now." He did that because he knew that Hubert Humphrey would win the election if peace was made. He was willing to perpetuate the war, which it did for years and the draft was even expanded. All those people killed just so he could win the election.

It was just an astoundingly wicked thing to do.

Right, which is astounding and which is so awful that he would do that.

Just to be clear, for people who aren't familiar with this, this isn't a conspiracy theory or something. This is recorded American history. This happened.

Right, and I did not know about it until I started researching this book because I had abandoned all interest in the Vietnam War movement after he failed. I just considered it one of those great failures that we didn't stop the war.

Then when I started researching it and I found all the information, their archival materials and documents would show that he ordered the peace process to be stalled and it was all done to keep the Democrats from making peace. He, in fact, then won the election. The war went on, into '73, '74, then he was able to end the draft and then he claimed that he succeeded in ending the war.

The impeachment of Nixon was of course, different from our talk about impeaching Trump, because he in fact obstructed justice in a criminal case that was in the courts here, the Watergate burglary, which involved crimes.

Other presidents had done this before, had taped things in the White House, but we didn't know about it at the time. He interfered with a criminal case in the court by suppressing information and obstructing justice clearly. On the night when he fired the prosecutors over at the Justice Department, who were special prosecutors, I went with my friend to Lafayette Park. Nobody was around and we started yelling, "Resign! Resign! Resign!"

Pretty soon, a crowd gathered outside the White House yelling for him to resign. It took some time, but he did.

Many people hope or expect the Trump presidency to follow that route. It seems like the left is always looking for magic bullets. Who knows? I don't put anything past Trump, but no, we're going to have to do the hard work of defeating his policies through activism and then the hard work of defeating his administration at the ballot box. There's no deus ex machina here, right?

As I said before, even if we got rid of him, there would be Pence, who would be much more able to implement the things that Trump is trying to do because he is an old political hand and knows better how to do things without leaving tracks and creating great controversy. That doesn't mean that the policy would change.

What we should focus on, as I write about in my book, is the policies and changing them. Black Lives Matter focuses on an issue. You don't have to be concerned about what the issue is. They now have come up with an agenda that has lots of issues, but when they started out, they were focused on police abuse of unarmed people. This is an issue which is easily understood even though it's difficult to resolve.

Earlier there was the Americans with Disabilities Act, passed by a coalition of movement people. That movement had a wonderful strategy of focusing on what they wanted to do, how to do it, how to change tactics and strategies. They did a wonderful job.

I think that the pro-choice marches that took place in the late eighties and the early nineties leading up to the *Pennsylvania v. Casey* decision were really well thought out. Marches usually don't change anything and especially don't if it's a one-off.

But they had waves of huge marches in Washington. I recall that Justice Scalia said that the court didn't pay any attention to people marching outside their windows. I said to my students, "If they don't pay attention, how do they know they're marching outside their windows?" They obviously did pay attention and it's clear that Justice O'Connor and Justice Kennedy were influenced by the huge succession of marches.

Further Reading

Berry, Mary Frances. *History Teaches us to Resist: How Progressive Movements Have Succeeded in Challenging Times*. Beacon Press 2018.

12

Political Corruption and Citizenship

Zephyr Teachout

I first met Zephyr Teachout in the course of working in New York politics. I was at Working Families Party when she ran for governor of the state, so I first encountered her as a political candidate before I became familiar with her academic and issue-based work.

I had interreacted with, by that point, hundreds of political candidates. It's fair to say Zephyr is the first person I've ever met who seems to genuinely enjoy running for office. Many politicians like being in office (and some don't even like that), but almost all view the huge amount of work that is needed to get there as, at best, a necessary grind. That Zephyr did not is (thought it might not at first seem like it) a huge testament to her character, her openness to meeting new people, her passion, dedication, and genuine belief in public service.

That is, in a sense, what this final conversation is about: the character we want our politicians to have. The character we, as citizens, need to have in order to maintain a democratically free republic. We started our conversation discussing the problem of political corruption in America, one of her academic areas of expertise, and how inimical it is to those goals.

Zephyr Teachout is Associate Law Professor and has taught at Fordham Law School since 2009. She was a death penalty defense lawyer at the Center for Death Penalty Litigation in North Carolina, and cofounded a nonprofit dedicated to providing trial experience to new law school graduates. She is known for her pioneering work

Zephyr Teachout, *Political Corruption and Citizenship* In: *What is Freedom?*. Edited by: Toby Buckle, Oxford University Press. © Oxford University Press 2021. DOI: 10.1093/oso/9780197572214.003.0013 in internet organizing, and was the first national Director of the Sunlight Foundation.

She has written dozens of law review articles and essays and two books. Her book *Corruption in America: From Benjamin Franklin's Snuff Box to Citizens United* was published by Harvard University Press in 2014 and is considered the most important modern work on the topic.

In 2014, Teachout ran for the Democratic Party's nomination for governor of New York against incumbent Andrew Cuomo. Though she ultimately lost, her stronger-than-expected showing with 31% of the vote revitalized the progressive movement in the state and helped lay the foundation for a leftward shift in its politics on issues like banning fracking and raising the state minimum wage.

You've argued that the problem of money in politics isn't new and doesn't start with *Citizens United*. What's the legal history that led us to this point?

It really starts, I would say, in 1976 with *Buckley v. Vallejo*, which was one of the first big cases that found that spending money in elections was protected First Amendment speech. What the case did is set up this way of thinking about cases involving regulations of campaign spending. It said we have a two-step process: Step one is we want to figure out whether the First Amendment is implicated at all. And then, if the First Amendment is implicated, the only kind of situation in which we can allow for any kind of rules regarding spending around campaigns, is if those rules are designed to serve anticorruption purposes.

It's a very hastily written per curiam opinion that has a whole bunch of problems, but the two-step structure that it created unwittingly, then set up a major fight for the next forty years about the meaning of corruption. Because, if the only reason you could justify limiting how much somebody can contribute to a campaign (say capping at $5,000 instead of unlimited contributions) is anticorruption, then it really matters what corruption means.

So the court wandered into a political philosophy fight, I think unwittingly. Then you see forty years of fights about what is, and is not corruption. I think it also led to a lot of academic dishonesty.

As a nonlegal person, I have this expectation that Supreme Court decisions are rigorously based in precedent. In these cases though, a great deal of the jurisprudence hangs on invented-for-the-occasion definitions and distinctions—or am I being uncharitable?

I think being uncharitable is correct. For instance, one of the things that really gets me worked up is this shift in defining corruption: That which is corruption is only quid pro quo corruption.

And if I said that to any group of people, people would probably nod their heads. It's Latin, it sounds very serious, it sounds like it comes from somewhere, right? Well, quid pro quo does not show up in corruption law before the 1970s. It's just not part of corruption law. It's a central part of contract law, expressing the idea of the relative equality of exchange; I give you this in exchange for that.

It actually enters the corruption lexicon, not through state court cases, trying to deal with bribed local officials, but through the Supreme Court, which has this idea. They first introduce quid pro quo corruption, and then refer to it persistently for the next thirty years as if it's an established thing. People, even people who disagree with *Citizens United*, have a sense that there is a long tradition of understanding the core of bribery law as being about quid pro quo corruption. And they use quid pro quo as if it has always been a sort of language set tied to corruption. It hasn't. What I think it does, and I say this jokingly and seriously, is I think it gives people a sense of clarity. Like, just using the Latin, you feel like there's clear boundaries.

Well if you have a Latin phrase it must be correct, right?

Right!? (Laughs) I'm serious though, because even those courts that do use the phrase quid pro quo, there's no clear contours of what's quid pro quo and what's not. And so, as one of the circuit courts quipped, "all quids are not made of the same stuff." You would actually see in federal bribery law (which has in the last few decades incorporated the language of quid pro quo, from the Supreme Court, not from statutes) there's been a huge range of different ways to think about what constitutes this very specific sounding, but in reality hard to apply, phrase.

So if corruption as quid quo pro, an explicit exchange of money for a vote, is a comparatively modern definition, how was it understood earlier in American history?
A good deal of the book is focused on the way in which the framers of the American Constitution thought about corruption. One thing, which is prior to everything else, it's just how much they thought about it: It was seen as an essential, fundamental, ongoing threat. I sometimes think they saw it like this is going to be the game of whack-a-mole we will be playing as a country forever. We have to always keep alert to the multiple ways in which self-governing politics can be corrupted, and corruption is the fundamental threat of a Republic.

I think that's really important to raise, maybe that seems obvious in 2016, but in 2010, when I started writing *Corruption in America*, the Supreme Court, I felt, was often treating corruption like it was like a problem of people stealing too many metal pipes, like a small criminal law problem, not a major structural problem. I think great wisdom of the framing era is this sense that as Hamilton said at the constitutional convention, we erected every practicable obstacle to corruption. You sort see this in this hot summer in Philadelphia, that as a question comes up, whether it be, how the electoral college is going to work or, the size of the Senate, or the number that took to veto, every question went through the wringer of what structural system is more or less likely to lead to corruption.

So number one is, is just how obsessed they were with corruption as the threat. Number two is that they had an understanding of corruption, which is that it's when those in public power use that public power for private narrow, selfish ends. They weren't talking about explicit bribes. There are few examples, and in fact, there weren't criminal law statutes against lawmakers being bribed at the time.

The framers, as most historians of the time will tell you, were students of Montesquieu, and Montesquieu was very much known as the anti-Hobbes; as rejecting Hobbes, his understanding of human nature. The key difference is people saw Hobbes as fundamentally egotistical. Montesquieu and the framers saw people as containing within themselves the possibilities for great benevolence, but also possibilities for great greed and selfishness. The task of structure building was to build structures that made it more likely that our capacities for public love would be cultivated and our tendency to greed would be discouraged.

So it's not an idea that all people are angels, nor an idea that all people are devils. It's rather an idea that all people have angels and devils within them. And the job of constitutional design is to make it as likely that the public orientation would be supported and cultivated.

A lot of people will say, partially quoting Madison, "we have a constitution that's made for a system of devils." This is actually a simplification of what certainly Montesquieu, which is where we get the phrase "separation of powers," thought he was doing, but also of what the founders thought that they were doing. In that if you take Hobbes, he actually didn't believe corruption as I described it, was possible, because he thought people were always private-facing in a certain sense. So the idea that you could be deterred from being public-facing is a kind of no brainer.

Adrian Blau said, it's not that Hobbes and Montesquieu disagreed about corruption. It's just that Aristotle's understanding of corruption was incoherent to Hobbes. It actually doesn't make sense given his definition of human nature.

That's a pretty key distinction on how you justify our system of government. It's not just guarding against the bad, it's also the drawing out of the good in human beings.

There's this persistently misquoted or mischaracterized Madisonian quote, where he says, "if we had a nation of angels that we'd have no need of government"; and people then infer from that we have a nation of devils. Of course, that isn't what he's saying. He's saying something extremely different, and nobody is more consistent than Madison on the need to cultivate good character, public facing character, and to dissuade greed.

What really flows from this is the idea of temptation; the language of temptation is everywhere because temptation really matters if you have a view of people being good or bad.

If you see human nature as deeply flexible, and you're compassionate about those who might be tempted, then you say, okay, we may not be able to get rid of temptations, but let's make it really complicated and difficult. Let's make a lot of hurdles that you have to jump over to do that dangerous or tempting thing. I actually think that it's a compassionate approach because it's saying we are all subject to temptation, so instead of testing us at all times, why don't we just make it really hard to work for the King instead of working for our constituents?

As the legal understanding of corruption has changed, has the view of human nature grounding it also changed?
When Sandra Day O'Connor, the last person with real political experience, left the court, suddenly corruption law changed. And I don't think it's a coincidence. I think she's the least abstract, and really understood what happens in politics.

There's now an idea of politicians as competent rational maximizers. In fact they're far more of a mess for good and ill; ethical and passionate, full of mistakes, full of opportunities, driven by courage and fear: outsized fear and outsized courage. All those things come to bear. I do think that once you have a societal vision of politicians as rational, egotistical, maximizers it can be self-fulfilling, as the culture at large expects you to serve donors and then the party starts to expect that. Then it becomes a self-reinforcing cycle.

The court has different elements in it, but certainly there is an element of the court that has a very thin understanding of human nature, and a very thin understanding of politics. That part of the court was dominant in *Citizens United* and the precursor decisions. I think that understanding both misses the potential altruism, public focus, and ideology of politicians and misses the incredible corrupting power of things that aren't explicit exchanges. So it just misses the mark on human nature in two major ways.

The other thing that comes along with that view is it's not just structures, it's also about values and culture. If, for instance, I went from a salary negotiation to taking my place on a jury everything about my psychology, motivation, and approach to the situation would change. That's about culture as much as it's about structures.

Yeah, that's exactly right, and it's why history matters so much, and why calling on the better parts of our history matters so much. Fantastic example, but if you wandered into a jury constructed by a historical neoliberalism, you would expect that jurors would be, if not told otherwise, sneaking out and seeing how this verdict might affect their stock prices.

You can make it even more perverse: A pure rational self-interest theorist might design a system where jurors were given financial incentives for better deliberations.

Right? And that will only lead to something terrible. It also underestimates our capacities when we are engaged in solving a public problem. One of the analogies that I use in the book is this idea that we, as a society, with a few minor exceptions, accept as unproblematic and normal, the idea that people care profoundly for their family. That doesn't mean they're self-harming, that they will do anything for their family; they'll care deeply for their family and still stay healthy. We understand that society has been structured in a way that supports this and encourages good parenting, being a good spouse, and a good member of a larger family unit.

A lot of the ways in which we think about a good public servant are very similar: A good public servant is not starving themselves, is healthy, enjoys a glass of wine if that's what they like to do, good music, and friends. But at the heart of their decision-making around their job will be what bridge, what roads, what school system is gonna serve the public? I know I am imperfect, I know my information is limited, but I'm going to do everything I can to serve the public.

That emotional state, that orientation of the spirit, is something we're really comfortable with in families. I think historically, certainly in the founding era, I would argue up to the 1970s, and for the man on the street up to the current day, is something we rightly expect of our public officials and feel betrayed when they don't have it.

Do you think people still do think of their politicians that way?

I'm trying to explain the feeling of betrayal that so many people have. You wouldn't have a feeling of betrayal, you might have anger, but not betrayal if you didn't think public servants were supposed to be public-oriented.

I think there is still some civic spirit, and in some ways there's a remarkable amount. As a politician, I can tell you that when you get in a group of fifteen people just sitting around and talking, the question very quickly can turn to what should we do? Not what should we do that will most serve me, but what should we as a collective? It's a language, it's a conversation that people are very comfortable with in certain settings.

I think that's from hundreds of years of history. I think that history matters. I think that civic culture is really hard to build and we shouldn't throw it away easily. At the same time, I think we're losing it fast.

How do you think progressives should feel about the political units of which they are a part? There's some on the left who just reject them entirely; who see America as founded in slavery and genocide, think it's been entirely bad since then, and that its total destruction, along with that of capitalism, would be something to be welcomed.
On the other hand you have a rightwing, chest-thumping, patriotism that I can't avail myself of either.
Those aren't the only two options!
Maybe first I should say where I come from; I'm a Langston Hughes patriot. Langston Hughes in this amazing poem, "Let America Be America Again," in the 1940s writes this really powerful exhortation about our relationship to history, where he says:

Let America be the dream the dreamers dreamed—
    Let it be that great strong land of love
    Where never kings connive nor tyrants scheme
    That any man be crushed by one above.

Then he says, and often actually this is what the quotation stops with, "America was never America to me," which fits into the story you're telling. But that's not where he goes, where he goes is I promise America will be:

Sure, call me any ugly name you choose—
    The steel of freedom does not stain.
    From those who live like leeches on the people's lives,
    We must take back our land again,
    America!
    O, yes,
    I say it plain,

America never was America to me,
And yet I swear this oath—
America will be!

What I think he's doing is he's rejecting two different versions of history, both of which are extremely toxic. One is, it was perfect before and we should try to regain it, (personally, I don't want to live in the 1850s or even the 1950s, that sounds terrible) but also he rejects the radical rejection of the better parts of American history.

I won't speak for Hughes, but I'll speak for myself: I want people to understand how bad it can get, what a totalitarian regime looks like, what it looks like when you really don't trust, even imperfectly, property rights or each other. Or don't believe that, even imperfectly, you can touch the levers of power. What it feels like if you close the window, because you're worried that you'll get arrested, if you speak negatively about the King. Like the view of human nature (some see it as all bad, some see it as all good, and I tend to think it's much more flexible) I think that history is also flexible.

There certainly is a strong tendency toward oligarchy, however, and that the rejection of a tradition that has extraordinary egalitarian strains within it is incredibly dangerous. It's like bombing Libya and expecting that Libya will suddenly become a democracy. I think that rejection, this is the way in which I am a deep, small-C conservative, can be extremely careless and selfish. I think it actually betrays either cruelty or real naïveté about how bad things can get.

There are horrific times in American history and I think it's hard, but necessary, to both acknowledge the horror and pull out the wisdom that accompanies that horror. Unless you have a sort of a deep, and I would say naïve, progressivism that the arc of history bends toward justice all by itself. I actually think that a lot of my generation, left and right, was overly influenced by the fall of the Berlin wall, which led to a kind of eleven-year triumphalism.

If the maintenance and expansion of freedom requires both our active participation and us being a certain type of person, being oriented in a certain way, what does that look like? What are the ways we can be good citizens?

I think it's really hard, because I think there's multiple ways to be a good citizen, there's not just one way. For a society to survive, you need a lot of citizens who are engaged in local politics. That doesn't mean that you can never engage in the most exciting Senate race in the world, or in a national day of action.

That's an incredibly important political statement. But those alone, even multiplied times million, will never be enough if you do not actually have local people involved in local politics.

What does that look like? Should we be going to town halls? What should we be doing?

This is a brain breaker for me: I both really believe it and I don't see how it happens, so it's a puzzle. First, is just to actually be reading local news, and actually choosing to seek that out, and you're shaking your head...

I'm shaking my head because I'm realizing I'm guilty of this myself: I read so much news and almost all of it is national, or at least state level.

Right! We are all expecting somebody else to do the local work, and I think this is one of the real puzzles. I actually think a real question then is; is this possible without devolving more power to the local level? Because I actually do think that learning often follows power, as opposed to exhortation.

So, one idea is people will learn more if they are told to learn more, and another is they'll learn more if they're in a position where their learning matters, or they feel like their learning matters. It's something I think about a lot. I don't know all the answers on this one.

The other thing is getting involved in groups. It's very hard, not impossible, but it's hard to be a citizen alone. And groups are like work! They're annoying! There's that one person who's always bringing up that crazy topic!

If there's a way in which the far right and the far left have joined, it's in an individualism, in seeing group membership as expressive, as opposed to a job. If you see your membership as expressive and your group does something annoying, then you quit. If you see group membership as a role, you stick with it.

I'm talking, in part, about the Democratic Party here: It's not that the Democratic Party expresses who I am. I think it is absolutely essential that the democratic party exists, and I'm going to do every damn thing I can on a local level to help make it really work.

Something else the left needs to stop saying is that the main parties are just as bad as each other. They're really not.

They're not even close!

The depth of cynicism and cruelty of the modern Republican Party, in what the party has already been able to do, and what it can do. In terms of the sickness that people will feel. The literal sickness, the physical pain, the loss, the despair that the Republican Party is wrecking on people is totally unacceptable.

I have my fights with the leadership in the Democratic Party. I'm not shy about them. But I think it's really important to be inside of something that we are trying to improve instead of outside something that has kind of scrolled past us.

The assumption of individual, rational self-interest really gets into everything doesn't it? If I'm approaching group membership asking what I'll get out of it, or how it allows me to express myself, or how it validates how I see myself, there's not going to be much reason to join a group. But that's not the only way we can understand who we are.

I get obsessed with this little tool called N-Gram viewer, it roughly, inaccurately, tracks the use of language in books over time. The other day I went and looked up "courage" and "incentive." As you might expect, "courage" has declined over the last hundred years in usage and "incentive" has vastly grown. They're not theoretically incompatible, but they both start with fundamentally different ideas of what a human is.

If courage is part of your daily conversation, you then think of your jobs and your roles differently. If incentive is part of your daily conversation, then you think of your jobs and your roles differently. Incentive not necessarily implies, but hints at, a kind of mechanistic human understanding. Whereas courage hints at us having these capacities that we might tap into. That's not denying self-interest; if people want to make a little money, that's fine. It's just that there's a thinness, a simplicity to it.

I do really love the jury example, because on a jury it's as if people just forget this story of what they are supposed to be for ten days, or two weeks. Then, when you don't have individual egotism dominating everything, there's a richness that can come in to replace it: There's confusion, there's anger, it's not simple; it's not just replaced by a thin idea of virtue, but a much more complex and rich human character comes in to take that place.

Further Reading

Teachout, Zephyr. *Corruption in America: From Benjamin Franklin's Snuff Box to Citizens United*. Harvard University Press 2016.

Acknowledgments

As the editor of this volume the responsibility for any mistakes or failures lies with me. I cannot however take sole credit, or anything like it—many people contributed to this project and I would like to close by acknowledging some of them.

This book would not have been possible without the *Political Philosophy Podcast*. The podcast would not have been possible without its audience. My first debt of gratitude is with them. I am genuinely grateful for everyone who has listened to episodes, subscribed, given me feedback via email or social media, shared the podcast online or recommended to friends, and supported the project monetarily through donations or buying merchandise. You have been an ineliminable part of creating a public platform for political philosophy that has brought deep engaged conversations to hundreds of thousands of people for free, and advertisement free. You have also, through supporting that project, made this book possible.

The podcast was also made possible by its guests. Academics, activists, journalists, and politicians who took the time for an extended discussion, with an often overly opinionated interviewer, for no other reward than making their expertise available to others. In the context of this volume I would particularly like to thank Cécile Fabre, the podcast's first-ever guest, who agreed to record some episodes with me when the show was simply an idea. Professor Fabre very generously gave me her thoughts and advice throughout the process from concept, to drafting the book proposal, to finding a publisher. Her assistance was absolutely invaluable in taking this project from idea to reality.

Needless to say, the book could not have happened without its amazing contributors. It is no exaggeration to say this volume has brought together many of most qualified people in the world to discuss this topic. I thank all of them for agreeing to have their interviews featured in this volume. I'm further grateful for the support many of them gave in editing their chapters, often through multiple drafts. The result is infinitely stronger thanks to their active participation.

In addition to the contributors, I also thank my wonderful mother, Linda Buckle, and my sister, Dora Buckle, for reading drafts and giving me edits and feedback. Having an outside perspective on how the chapters read, whether our conversions to written English made sense, and whether our presentation of the issues was accessible, was incredibly useful. Similarly, I'm grateful to Peter Adamson for discussing how to introduce the volume. I also thank Peter Olin from Oxford University Press for taking an interest in the project and always being responsive and helpful as I put the manuscript together.

Finally, this project happened at a strange personal time for me. I started work on the manuscript in New York when the city was at the height of its coronavirus curve and nobody knew just how bad it might get. I finished it in the UK after a long-planned move made all the more difficult, and to some degree more dangerous, by the crisis. I'd like to acknowledge the person I did all of this with; my wife and life partner, Irina Tavera. Love you, babes.

List of Contributors

Editor: Toby Buckle, Podcast Host.

Cécile Fabre, Senior Research Fellow at All Souls College, Oxford, and Professor of Political Philosophy at the University of Oxford.

Elizabeth Anderson, Arthur F. Thurnau Professor and John Dewey Distinguished University Professor of Philosophy and Women's Studies at the University of Michigan.

Mary Frances Berry, Geraldine R. Segal Professor of American Social Thought, University of Pennsylvania.

Ian Dunt, Journalist and author. Editor at Large for politic.co.uk, Collumist for the New European and the I, contributor to a variety of Newspapers Magazines and websites, and author.

Michael Freeden, Professorial Research Associate, the School of Oriental and African Studies, University of London. Also Emeritus Professorial Fellow at Mansfield College, Oxford.

Nancy Hirschmann, Professor of Politics, University of Pennsylvania.

Omar Khan, Director TASO, Formerly Director of the Runnymede Trust.

Dale Martin, Woolsey Professor of Religious Studies (retired), Yale University.

Orlando Patterson, John Cowles Professor of Sociology at Harvard University.

Phillip Pettit, Laurance S. Rockefeller University Professor of Politics and Human Values, Princeton University. Also Distinguished University Professor of Philosophy, Australian National University.

John Skorupski, Professor of Moral Philosophy, University of St Andrews.

Peter Tatchell, Activist. Human rights campaigner, Director of the Peter Tatchell Foundation.

Zephyr Teachout, attorney, political candidate, associate professor of law, Fordham University.

Index

For the benefit of digital users, indexed terms that span two pages (e.g., 52–53) may, on occasion, appear on only one of those pages.

1 Corinthians, 34, 39, 42–43
1 Thessalonians, 34
2 Corinthians, 34

Acts of the Apostles, 33–34, 37, 39, 40
Amazon, 109
Americans with Disabilities Act, 192
Astell, Mary, 80
Atlee, Clement, 2, 66

Bentham, Jeremy, 90, 94–95, 105
Berlin, Isaiah, 74–75, 76–77, 85–86
Beveridge report, 63, 170
Black Lives Matter, 192
Blair, Tony, 135, 161, 168, 177, 180
Blau, Adrian, 197
Boeing, 123–24
Brexit, 7, 159, 160, 163, 172–73, 174–75, 178–80
Buckley v. Vallejo, 194

Calhoun, John, C, 124–25
Calvin, John, 49
Cameron, David, 150, 176
Carlyle, Thomas, 94–95
Cato, the elder, 28
Citizens United V. FEC, 194, 195, 199
Clinton, Bill, 124, 188–89
Clinton, Hillary, 186
Coleridge, Samuel Taylor, 94–95
Constantine, 48
constraint
   constitutional, 107–8
   on corporate power, 122–23
   cultural, 53–54
   deontic, 103–4

moral, 57, 97–98
non-constraint, 4–5, 54–55, 57, 86, 157
racism/ Sexism as, 156–57, 164
corruption, 195–97, 198
Cromwell, Oliver, 131–32

Douglass, Fredrick, 132

Eisenhower, Dwight, 182, 183
Erasmus, 49
essential contestability, 1–2, 53–54, 55–56
Euripides, 28
European Union, 162, 172, 174–77, 178–79
Eusebius, 48

Facebook, 109
Finley, Mosses, 27
Floyd, George, 164
Foucault, Michel, 76–77
Friedan, Betty, 83

Galatians, 34, 35, 36, 45
Gerald Cohen, Gerald, 74–75
Graham, Billy, 95

Hamilton, Alexander, 196
Hayek, Friedrich, 64, 65, 169
Hobbes, Thomas, 74, 78, 197
Hobhouse, Leonard, 55, 61–63
Hobson, John, 55, 61–63
Horace, 29–30
Hughes, Langston, 201–2
Humboldt, Wilhelm Von, 94

Ibsen, Henrik, 105–6, 107–8
ideology, 2, 3, 21, 25–26, 54, 56, 58, 60,
    61, 62–63, 65, 66, 80, 83–85, 168,
    169–70, 199
Immigration Aliens Acts of 1905, 151
Immigration and Nationality Act of
    1948, 151
individualism, 4–5, 8, 46, 49, 59, 76–77,
    94, 102, 115, 154, 155, 164–65,
    167, 204
individuality, 5–6, 57, 59, 92

Jefferson, Thomas, 31
Jesus
    body of, 39–40
    followers, 40
    freedom in, 46–47
    historical, 37–40
    resurrection, 38–39
John, Gospel of, 38
Johnson, Boris, 161

Kant, Immanuel, 78
Kennedy, Anthony, 192
Keynes, J M, 66, 169
King, Martin Luther, 145, 152–53

law
    anti-corruption, 195–97, 198
    concept of, 112–13, 116
    discrimination in, 88, 105–6, 111, 136,
        137, 140, 145–46, 148, 151
    economic, 65–66
    equality under, 145, 146
    Roman, 19–20
    trade & anti-trust, 109, 113, 173
Levellers, the, 131
liberty principle, 57, 58, 90–91, 92, 96–97
Lincoln, Abraham, 1, 125
Lloyd George, David, 63–64
Locke, John, 56–57, 78
Luke, Gospel of, 37, 38, 39
Luther, Martin, 49
Luxemburg, Rosa, 148

MacCallum, Gerald, 54, 59–60
Madison, James, 197, 198

Madison, James, 197, 198
Mark, Gospel of, 37, 38, 39
marriage, 83–84, 116, 137–40, 148
Matthew, Gospel of, 38
May, Theresa, 150
Mill, Harriet Taylor, 171
Mill, James, 90, 171
Mill, John Stuart
    childhood, 90, 171
    economic views, 170–71
    experiments in living, 95
    free speech 171, 173–74
    general references, 2, 55, 56, 61, 78, 90
    harm, 91
    individual self-development, 57, 58, 59,
        92, 93–95, 170
    liberty principle, 57, 58, 90–91,
        92, 96–97
    moral constraints, 97–98
Mills, Charles, 130
Milton, John, 112
Montesquieu, 1, 197–94
Musk, Elon, 123

negative liberty, 5–6, 25, 58, 59, 73,
    74–75, 76–77, 78–79, 84, 85,
    87, 156
Nixon, Richard, 189–91
non-domination, 8, 18, 25, 100, 106–8,
    109, 112, 113–14, 116, 130
Nozick, Robert, 102–3

O'Connor, Sandra Day, 192, 198
Obama, Barack, 124
open borders, 161–62
OutRage!, 147

Paul, 33–37, 38–40, 41–43, 45–46, 47–
    48, 49–51
Pennsylvania v. Casey, 192
Philemon, 34
Philippians, 34
Philo, 28
Plato, 22, 43
polygamy / polyamory, 98
positive liberty, 5–6, 73, 75, 85–87
Putney debates, 131–32

racism, 75, 82, 86, 124, 127–28, 145, 153–
  55, 157, 158, 159–61, 163–65
rational choice, 1, 58–59, 80, 154, 155,
  198–99, 204
Rawls, John, 67–69, 93
Reagan, Ronald, 182–83, 184, 185
Ricardo, David, 170–71
Romans, 34, 35–36, 42, 45
Rousseau, 75, 78

Scalia, Antonin, 192
Schiller, Friedrich, 94
Sen, Amartya, 26
sex education, 140–43
sexism, 75, 83–84, 86, 157, 165
slavery
  American, 2, 30, 124–25, 132, 163, 201
  ancient near east, 20, 27, 43–44, 48
  British role, 15, 161, 163
  Caribbean, 15–16
  in Christianity, 42, 45–47
  definition, 16–17, 46–33, 153
  Greek, 3, 20, 21–26, 43, 44, 47
  pre-settled, 17–19
  Roman, 3, 20, 23, 28–30, 42–43, 44–45,
    48, 107–1
Smith, Adam, 113–15, 170–71
social construction, 67, 79–82, 83–
    85, 86, 87
  paradox of 82
Spencer, Herbert, 55

Taylor, Charles, 76–77
Thatcher, Margret, 2, 66
Thomas, Gospel of, 38
Trump, Donald, 43–44, 124, 126, 160,
    166, 172, 180, 183, 186–88, 189, 191
Tupinambra, 19

United Kingdom, politics of
  Brexit, 7, 159, 160, 163, 172–73, 174–
    75, 178–80
  Civil War, 131
  decolonization, 15–16, 21, 28, 149–50,
    151–52, 154
  imperial period, 15–16, 161, 163, 170
  New Labour, 135, 160, 161, 168, 177
  postwar consensus, 66–67
  Thatcher revolution, 2, 66,
    67, 169–70
  welfare state, 2, 63–65, 66, 155
United States Commission on Civil
    Rights, 182–83
United States, politics of
  civil war, 1, 128, 132
  Clinton 124, 188–89
  Eisenhower, Dwight, 182, 183
  founding, 1, 30, 31, 67, 105, 196, 197,
    198, 200
  Nixon, Richard, 189–91
  Reagan, 182–83, 184, 185
  segregation/ civil rights, 2–3, 145, 155,
    182–83, 188, 189–90
  Trump, 43–44, 124, 126, 160, 166, 172,
    180, 183, 186–88, 189, 191
utilitarianism, 90, 93, 94–95,
    105, 170–71

war
  Jamaican Slave Revolt, 16
  UK Civil, 131
  US Civil, 1, 128, 132
  Vietnam War, 190
  World War One, 65
  World War Two, 68, 149–50, 174
welfare state, 2, 63–65, 66, 111, 155, 189
Wollstonecraft, Mary, 80–81